The Teacher's Guide to

Grammar

The Teacher's Guide to
Grammar

Deborah Cameron

OXFORD
UNIVERSITY PRESS

OXFORD
UNIVERSITY PRESS

Great Clarendon Street, Oxford OX2 6DP

Oxford University Press is a department of the University of Oxford.
It furthers the University's objective of excellence in research, scholarship,
and education by publishing worldwide in

Oxford New York

Auckland Cape Town Dar es Salaam Hong Kong Karachi
Kuala Lumpur Madrid Melbourne Mexico City Nairobi
New Delhi Shanghai Taipei Toronto

With offices in

Argentina Austria Brazil Chile Czech Republic France Greece
Guatemala Hungary Italy Japan Poland Portugal Singapore
South Korea Switzerland Thailand Turkey Ukraine Vietnam

Oxford is a registered trade mark of Oxford University Press
in the UK and in certain other countries

British Library Cataloguing in Publication Data

Data available

Typeset by Graphicraft Limited, Hong Kong
Printed in Italy by Legoprint S.P.A.

ISBN 978-0-19-921448-8

1 3 5 7 9 10 8 6 4 2

Contents

Acknowledgements

The examples of school pupils' writing which are reproduced in this book were collected from schools in the London area in 2005–6 by PGCE students at the Institute of Education, London. I gratefully acknowledge the assistance of these students, the schools they worked in, and the pupils themselves. I am particularly indebted to Anne Turvey at the Institute, not only for helping me to obtain writing samples, but also for her advice on the book and her comments on draft chapters. I also thank her colleagues Anton Franks and John Yandell, Bethan Marshall of King's College London, and Janet White.

Introduction

This is a book about the structure and workings of the English language. It is written for teachers and those preparing to become teachers, especially (though not exclusively) teachers of English.

English teachers have always made use of knowledge about the English language. But in recent years, developments such as the introduction of the national curriculum and national literacy strategy have made it necessary for them to draw on a more extensive and more formal linguistic knowledge. For many, this is a challenge, because the formal study of language has not been part of their own education. In audits of their subject-knowledge, beginning English teachers—a majority of whom are English literature graduates—often say that their biggest concern is how little they feel they know about grammar. This book is intended to address that concern: to help teachers feel more secure in their knowledge, and thus more confident in using and communicating what they know.

I am not the first writer to address this topic for this audience. The inclusion of grammar in the national curriculum has spurred people to produce all kinds of resources: quick reference guides to grammar and its terminology, sample lesson plans, suggested classroom activities. There are also various 'grammar made simple' books written for a general audience. But without denying that these can be useful (some of them are listed in the Further Reading section), this book sets out to do something different.

First, it makes the assumption that what teachers need to know about grammar is not limited to what the national curriculum requires them to teach about it. Clearly, teachers do need to be equipped with the knowledge they are expected to pass on to pupils, but in these pages I will try to demonstrate that an understanding of language structure is relevant not only for teaching grammar itself, but also for teaching writing, spelling, reading, literature, and media. It can also assist teachers in making informed and systematic assessments of pupils' language development, as part of the ongoing activity of monitoring their learning.

This activity may be less visible than actual classroom teaching, but it is every bit as important. With that in mind, most of the following chapters contain sections headed 'Looking at pupils' writing', where linguistic knowledge is used to reflect on real examples of written work produced by schoolchildren.

Second, this book is not just concerned with the what of grammar, but also with the why and the how. This differentiates it from most popular grammar-guides, which generally stick to presenting the facts as concisely as possible. For some purposes, that brevity is doubtless a virtue, but for the purposes of education it has certain limitations. In today's classrooms, it is generally accepted that there is more to learning than simply memorizing facts and definitions: learners are encouraged to ask questions, and to consolidate their understanding by applying their knowledge actively. If grammar is not to be an exception in this respect, teachers need to be able to explain the principles behind the facts, and show pupils how to use those principles to reason things out for themselves. That is also what I will try to do here.

Third, this book will acknowledge that grammar is a controversial subject, both in educational circles and in society more generally. Even as I write, a report has just been published by the Confederation of British Industry (and given blanket shock-horror coverage in the media), which calls for schools to pay more attention to grammar in order to stem what is presented as a rising tide of illiteracy in the nation's workplaces.[1] Grammar is often talked about in these terms, as a miracle cure for problems with reading, writing and spelling. This has done it no favours among teachers, whose experience tells them there are no easy solutions. I agree: though I am interested in what grammatical knowledge can help teachers do, I am not going to suggest that grammar is the answer to every problem. Grammatical knowledge is a tool: like any tool it is useful for some things and unnecessary or unsuitable for others. When it is useful, and how it can best be used, are matters for teachers' professional judgement. But teachers can only make informed judgements if they have some grammatical knowledge in the first place.

In chapter 1 we will take a closer look at educational debates on grammar, and at the more general social attitudes they reflect. Chapters 2–7 deal with various aspects of the structure of English,

and chapters 8–10 examine some issues relating to language variation.
At the end of the book there is a section containing suggestions for
further reading, and a glossary of technical terms (terms which appear in
the glossary are indicated in the text by bold type). These are unavoidable
in a book about grammar, since it is impossible to talk about any kind
of structure without having labels for its components; but most of the
terms I use are terms teachers need to become familiar with in any case,
since they are also used in national curriculum documents.

This is not a comprehensive guide to grammar aimed at academic
readers, nor a basic guide to grammar for the general reader, but
specifically a teacher's guide to grammar: it concentrates on those
aspects of grammar that are most relevant for teachers' purposes.
As I have already said, though, I have resisted defining those purposes
too narrowly. Rather than focusing exclusively on grammar teaching,
this book sets out to explore the larger question of what grammar
can contribute to English teaching. It begins, though, by considering
why that question—the question of grammar's place in English
teaching—has been, and still is, a cause of such conflict and
controversy

Grammar

I dread those occasions when I am forced to admit in public that my job involves teaching grammar. I know that as soon as I utter the g-word, some people will immediately start apologizing for their 'mistakes', or remarking that they will have to mind their language in my presence; others will feel the need to test my credentials with a challenging question about the **subjunctive** or the semicolon. Older people may recall some hideous sadist who taught them grammar at school, leaving me to wonder if they think I am cast in the same mould. Alternatively they may suggest that people like me are doing a very poor job compared to the sadists of yesteryear: 'so, why doesn't anyone nowadays know where to put an apostrophe?' Anxiety, self-abasement, defensiveness, aggression—what is it about grammar that sparks these reactions?

For most people, the word 'grammar' means 'rules for using a language correctly'. The rules are peremptory commands like 'never split an **infinitive**', 'two negatives make a positive', 'it's *we were*, not *we was*', 'don't say *aint*'. Over time these dos and don'ts have become shibboleths, distinguishing 'us' (who know and care about our grammar) from 'them' (the ignorant, lazy, and careless). Grammar has thus become associated with the idea of making negative judgements, not only on a person's speech or writing, but also by implication on their social status and moral worth. When even something as trivial as a single misplaced apostrophe can be used to condemn the person who misplaced it as 'illiterate', it is hardly surprising if people's attitudes to grammar are coloured by feelings of inadequacy, fear, and shame.

Attitudes to grammar are also influenced, even now, by its long history as a school subject and its association with a certain kind of pedagogy. Grammar was one of the subjects studied by children across medieval

Europe, but what it meant at that time was Latin grammar: it was taught to enable pupils to master the dead foreign language which was then a basic educational requirement. It was not until the 20th century that large numbers of English-speaking pupils encountered grammar in lessons dealing with their own language. But for many, it seems the instruction they received might just as well have been in Latin: the methods used were similar, and the content equally incomprehensible. In her memoir of life at a 1950s' girls' grammar school, the writer Mary Evans remembers many tedious hours spent underlining verbs in green and nouns in red.[1] With no idea what the point of this might be, the girls ended up, she records, with the vague impression that grammar worked rather like traffic lights.

The kind of grammar teaching Mary Evans describes was in decline by the 1970s, a casualty of changing social attitudes and new educational theories. But in the late 1980s, when the national curriculum was being planned, 'bring back grammar' became a rallying cry for a vocal lobby of cultural conservatives. These advocates regarded grammar as an antidote to the 'permissiveness' and 'sloppiness' that had taken root in education during the previous two decades. Prince Charles, for example, deploring the fact that English was 'taught so bloody badly' and demanding that this be remedied by the reintroduction of grammar lessons, explained: 'We must educate for character. . . . You cannot educate people properly unless you do it on a basic framework and drilling system'. The Conservative politician Norman Tebbit suggested that a lack of respect for what was right and wrong in language marked the beginning of a slippery slope that led inexorably to crime.[2]

In the light of all this, it is not hard to understand why so many contemporary English teachers view grammar with suspicion or hostility. To begin with, teachers are not immune to the feelings of inadequacy that any mention of grammar is liable to provoke. On the contrary, their profession makes them particularly vulnerable. Accusing teachers of 'illiteracy' is a favourite strategy of the media whenever they indulge in one of their periodic bouts of teacher-bashing: 'look, here's a school report written by a teacher who can't spell or punctuate'. Or 'look, here's a survey showing that x% of applicants for teacher training make basic grammatical errors'. Where no distinction is made between knowing about language and using it 'correctly', proposals to enhance teachers' understanding of grammar can all too easily be read as implying that teachers need remedial English lessons—an insult which is bound to be resented.

The association of grammar with 'correctness' on one hand and 'discipline' on the other also prompts opposition to its inclusion in the school curriculum. While most teachers accept the need to teach **standard English** (which is often equated with 'correct' English, though we will see later on that this begs certain questions), few see making negative judgements on pupils' own home languages and **dialects** as a useful strategy for achieving that aim. Nor would many agree with Prince Charles about the character-building virtues of grammatical drills. If teachers think that is what teaching grammar must entail, no wonder so many resist the idea.

But although there are good reasons to criticize the way grammar has been taught in the past, we should not assume that there is no other way to approach it. Traditional aims and methods were linked to a particular view of grammar itself as a *prescriptive* enterprise, one whose purpose was to instruct learners in the proper use of language. This definition of grammar still dominates popular common sense, but among experts it has long since yielded to an alternative view of grammar as *descriptive*—an investigation of how languages work and what their users are able to do with them. Failure to distinguish between these two views of grammar all too often leads to arguments in which the opposing sides are talking at cross purposes. But unless we are clear what we mean by the term 'grammar', we cannot make a proper assessment of its value for teachers or learners. With that in mind, I want to spend a little time exploring the difference between prescriptive and descriptive approaches.

Prescriptive grammar

The definition of grammar which I said earlier was accepted as common sense by most people—'rules for using a language correctly'—is in fact a definition of **prescriptive grammar**, so called because the rules *prescribe* what is correct (and/or *proscribe*—forbid—what is not correct). In the case of English, prescriptive grammar has its roots in the 18th century, a period language historians label 'the age of **codification**'.

To 'codify' is to set down some body of rules authoritatively and systematically: in this case, what was being codified was the vocabulary and grammar of English, and the results were dictionaries and grammar books. These were part of the long historical process of establishing a standard dialect of English: a form of the language with clearly defined rules, which could be taught, learnt, and used consistently throughout the country.

Language **standardization** is a somewhat artificial process, because its aim is to produce uniformity of usage, whereas in reality usage is not uniform, it is *variable*. This is not only a matter of there being different regional or social dialects of the language: even within one dialect there will often be two or more ways of saying the same thing, which speakers and writers alternate between. Thus in standard English 'everybody' and 'nobody' coexist with 'everyone' and 'no one'; if you tell me you are going out tonight, I can ask either 'who with?' or 'with whom?' This **optional variability** is normal in languages (and useful, since it allows us to choose different linguistic variants—for instance, more and less formal ones—to suit the needs of different situations), but it is in tension with the goal of making usage uniform. True uniformity requires just one of the forms in use to be selected as the standard. Though it is ultimately impossible to eradicate variation, codifiers sought to minimize it by handing down authoritative rulings on which of the competing forms was considered best.

Their judgements were often influenced by the fact that the language whose grammar they knew most about was not English but Latin. Men whose education had centred on the study of Latin found it natural to take Latin rules as their model for English ones, despite the structural differences between the two languages. One legacy of this is the long-lived proscription of split infinitives like 'to boldly go': in Latin the infinitive cannot be split, for the simple reason that it is a single word (e.g. *ire*, 'to go'). In English, that structural constraint does not exist, and the proscription is entirely artificial. So is the rule against ending a sentence with a preposition. There is no structural reason why you should not describe grammar as 'a subject I've never cared for' rather than 'a subject for which I've never cared'.

Another influence on prescriptive grammarians' choices was, bluntly, snobbery. If two competing forms were associated with the speech of different groups in society, codifiers would choose the one used by higher-status people. The proscription of the *double negative* (e.g. 'we didn't do nothing') is a case in point. Although it was justified then as now by an appeal to the laws of mathematics—'two negatives make a positive'—the real reason for proscribing it was that by 1700 it already carried a social stigma and was avoided by educated speakers.

This example illustrates the arbitrary nature of many rules—the fact that typically there is no linguistic, as opposed to social, motivation for preferring one form to another. The English double negative was perfectly correct in the Middle Ages: Chaucer, for instance, used it extensively. In modern French, the standard way of making a negative sentence calls for negation to be marked twice, as in *Je **ne** sais **pas***, 'I don't know', and *je **ne** sais **rien*** 'I (don't) know nothing'. In informal speech, French speakers today often omit the '*ne*', and this move from two negatives to one attracts disapproving judgements. If double negatives were good English in Chaucer's time and are still the more prestigious form in French, it becomes difficult to believe the 'official' explanation of why they are supposed to be avoided, that 'two negatives make a positive'. The laws of mathematics are invariant; what varies is the social distribution of different negative constructions.

Traditional prescriptive grammar, then, is not the best foundation for understanding how the English language works. Many prescriptive rules are peripheral to, or even at odds with, the basic structure of English, because they were made by people whose template for all grammar was Latin grammar. Prescriptive grammarians have often misleadingly presented what are really social value-judgements as facts about the English language, and defined 'correctness' in a way that ignores the need for stylistic flexibility. Another problem with prescriptive grammar is its selective coverage of the linguistic system. By concentrating so heavily on a small set of shibboleths that carry a lot of social baggage, the average prescriptive text leaves out more of the facts about grammar than it includes.

Over the last 30 years, educational policymakers have turned away from prescriptive grammar, not only because of the shortcomings just noted, but also for pedagogical reasons. In 1975 the influential Bullock Report questioned the priorities of the prescriptive approach, remarking that it placed emphasis 'less on knowing what to say than on knowing what to avoid'.[3] Since Bullock, professionals have generally taken the view that a competent language-user is not simply one who does not make mistakes in grammar, spelling or punctuation, but more importantly one who is able to communicate meaning effectively. One consequence, however, has been to put professional orthodoxy at odds with popular common sense. The public at large continues to believe that a writer's (in)competence can be measured simply by counting mistakes—hence all those news reports with headlines like 'Spelling mistakes and poor grammar cost UK business £700 million a year', 'Spelling and grammar howlers are the norm for graduate applications', and 'Sloppy spelling and grammar outrage in A-level examiners'.[4]

Concerns of this kind, particularly among employers, have recently led to proposals for a new test of GCSE students' *functional English*—in essence, their ability to avoid 'howlers'. Many teachers are uneasy about this apparent reversion to the old prescriptive approach and its obsession with knowing what to avoid. Without suggesting that mistakes do not matter at all (clearly they do, if only because so many people judge them so harshly), an approach in which avoiding mistakes is the only thing that matters overlooks the fact that, in Debra Myhill's words, 'weak writing cannot be crudely correlated with inaccuracy'.[5] Weak writers do make grammar and spelling errors, but when these are corrected the result is often not much better, because the writer's real problem goes deeper: s/he has problems conveying meaning in written language or designing text to meet the needs of a reader. We will look at some examples of these deeper problems in the pupils' writing I reproduce later: I think it will be evident that they cannot be solved using approaches which focus narrowly on surface correctness. But I will try to show how these problems might be illuminated by the systematic understanding of linguistic structure which is offered by the alternative, descriptive approach to grammar.

Descriptive grammar: structure and meaning

One objection to grammar that has sometimes been voiced by English teachers is that grammar is concerned with only the *formal* aspects of language, and so is not helpful in an approach that emphasizes using language to communicate meaning. In relation to prescriptive grammar this objection is clearly justified. The shibboleths that preoccupy prescriptive grammarians are all cases where the 'correct' and 'incorrect' usages are exactly equivalent in meaning: the difference between, say, *it ain't* and *it isn't* or *we was* and *we were* is purely a matter of surface form, and the meaning it conveys is social rather than linguistic. Teaching children to substitute 'isn't' for 'ain't' is like teaching them not to eat peas with a knife: it treats grammar as a kind of social etiquette.

But this objection cannot so readily be made to **descriptive grammar**. In a descriptive model, the 'rules' of grammar are not instructions specifying how language ought to be used, but generalizations describing how people who know a language actually do use it in practice. More specifically, they describe what users of a language know about the structure of that language—about how words, **phrases** and sentences are put together. The aim of descriptive grammar is to describe the structural principles that allow us to put linguistic units together in ways that mean something.

The importance of grammatical structure for meaning is sometimes overlooked or underestimated, because of the common-sense perception that meaning resides in words. And of course, words do make a crucial contribution to meaning. But so too does grammatical structure, for as Paul Tench explains:

> Whereas words represent the categorization of our experience of
> life in terms of entities . . . [grammar] represents our categorization
> of our experience of life in terms of happenings: who does what?
> And to whom (or what), and why, how, where, when?[6]

The meaningful ordering of experience in language is accomplished both by naming entities using words and by representing the states, processes or events those entities are involved in using the resources of grammatical form. For instance, 'who does what to whom' is generally conveyed in English by the ordering of the **subject**, verb, and **object** constituents in a sentence—think of those apocryphal headlines 'dog bites man' and 'man bites dog' (same three words, different order, completely different meaning). When things happened, and whether actions are completed or still ongoing, is conveyed by contrasts in the form of the verb—think of the differences between *I see it, I'm seeing it,*

I've seen it and *I saw it*. These formal distinctions are not just
meaningless: being able to manipulate them is part of being able
to express precisely what you mean.

If we move away from identifying grammar narrowly with accuracy or
correctness, it becomes possible to approach it as an aspect of meaning-
making, which as such is neither irrelevant to nor in conflict with the
priorities of most English teachers. But it might still be asked, 'why do
teachers need to master descriptive grammar, if all it describes is their
own behaviour? What will it tell them about English that they don't
already know? What can they do with it that they could not do just
as well without it?'

The uses of explicitness

My answer to these questions goes back to the distinction between
explicit knowledge and implicit, intuitive or *tacit* (unspoken) knowledge.
What we know about English grammar by virtue of being proficient users
of the language is tacit knowledge: although we follow rules, in most
cases we cannot state explicitly what they are. The rules most people
can state explicitly ('never split an infinitive', etc.) are not statements
describing the 'real' structure of English, but prescriptions which
artificially modify that structure. The descriptive study of grammar is
about bringing the 'real' rules to consciousness, so that they can be
described systematically.

But how does it help learners if teachers are able to do that? Here
the answer has to do with the nature of what schoolchildren have to
learn. Though it is true that even very young children have extensive tacit
knowledge about the grammar of their native tongues (the fundamentals
of a first language are normally acquired in the first few years of life),
it is not true that school pupils—even much older ones—already know
everything they need to know in order to use language in the particular
ways education demands. Schooling focuses on those areas of language-
use which do not just develop naturally. Mastering the written form of
the language is an obvious example; but it may not be obvious that there
is far more to this than just learning the script and the spelling system.
As we will see later, the grammatical structure of written English differs
in important ways from that of informal spoken English. Even the

concept of a sentence, which literate people think of as basic to all language, may not be intuitively obvious to someone not yet literate. Learning to read and write thus involves acquiring new grammatical resources. This process continues throughout schooling, as learners engage with the increasingly complex language that is needed to convey more complex knowledge. For many learners, too, becoming literate entails mastering a dialect of English, namely standard English, which is not the one they have already acquired. And for some learners, English is not their **first language**, and they will need support to become proficient in it.

One way in which teachers enable learners to develop as language-users is by providing them with *models*. Teachers model the standard dialect in their own speech and writing, and they model various aspects of written English grammar when they discuss learners' writing, correct errors and help writers see what choices they might make about how to convey certain meanings. Modelling does not depend on explicit linguistic knowledge. Rather it makes use of the teacher's intuitive knowledge and his/her own more highly developed skills as an experienced user of English. But there are cases where learners do not pick up on a general principle just by having examples of its operation modelled for them. Some learners find this easier to do than others; some principles are easier to intuit than others. Sometimes it is useful to be able to draw a learner's attention explicitly to what the underlying principle or rule is—to explain it as well as modelling it. That, however, does require explicit knowledge: you cannot explain a principle to someone else if you do not know yourself what it is.

For instance, some errors in writing reflect the influence of the learner's **non-standard** dialect of English. Case-by-case correction of the non-standard form (i.e. modelling the appropriate standard form) is not always effective, however, because the individual forms which are targets for correction belong to a larger grammatical system: what the learner has to come to understand is not simply the difference between two forms, but the difference between two systems, each with its own grammatical rules. If that systemic dimension is not addressed, the result may be to eliminate the original error, but at the cost of introducing a new one. The linguist Jenny Cheshire found in research she carried out in Reading that teachers generally corrected the local non-standard verb forms in sentences like *we goes into town on Saturdays*. Pupils learnt from this to substitute the standard form *we go* for the non-standard *we goes*. However, the generalization they deduced from teachers' corrections ('don't put *-s* endings on present **tense** verbs') was not the standard English rule, which does require *-s* endings on third **person** singular (he/she/it) verbs. Consequently, some pupils started writing things like *a hedgehog live in a hole*, which is neither standard English nor part of the local dialect.[7]

This is a case—in later chapters I will discuss others—where the ability to analyse language structure systematically has the potential to illuminate something about a learner's use of language: what s/he is able to do, what s/he is not yet doing, and what the errors s/he makes suggest about the reasoning s/he is currently using. This ongoing assessment of linguistic development is probably the most important purpose grammatical knowledge serves for teachers, and it would still be just as important if grammar were not part of the curriculum for their pupils. But of course, grammar *is* currently included in the curriculum that school pupils in England and Wales are required to follow. Whether it should be, however, is a matter of ongoing debate and controversy: both teachers and academic researchers have questioned whether teaching grammar explicitly to pupils serves any useful purpose.

In 1984 the researcher Katherine Perera noted that '. . . research has accumulated [showing] that grammatical instruction, unrelated to pupils' other language work, does not lead to an improvement in the quality of their own writing or in their level of comprehension'.[8] Two decades later, a team at the EPPI-Centre ('EPPI' stands for 'Evidence for Policy and Practice Information') undertook a fresh review of the evidence.[9] Their conclusion was that grammar teaching has no positive effect on pupils' writing. In the light of that, they criticized the national curriculum for compelling schools to spend time on an activity whose effectiveness was not supported by evidence.

In my own view, the evidence about grammar and writing is not as straightforward to interpret as the EPPI-Centre review implies. One problem is the mixed nature of the findings overall: other researchers assessing the evidence have reached the opposite conclusion from the EPPI-Centre, that grammatical instruction *can* enhance writing skills.[10] Another problem relates to Perera's point that grammatical instruction is ineffective where it is 'unrelated to pupils' other language work'. The EPPI-Centre did not consider whether the teachers in the studies they reviewed related grammar to writing. If they did not, that in itself might explain why pupils did not make the connection. The national curriculum does try to address this problem, by emphasizing the importance of an integrated approach.

The whole debate which the EPPI-Centre review is part of focuses on a single question: whether grammar teaching makes children better writers. Improving writing is by implication the only purpose teaching grammar in the classroom could possibly serve: if the evidence suggests that it does not serve that purpose, it is axiomatically a waste of time. But this narrow view of what grammatical knowledge is good for is not the only possible view, and not the one taken by the national curriculum. At this point we might want to look a little more closely at the national curriculum's view of grammar.

Grammar in the national curriculum

The national curriculum does assume that grammatical knowledge has a role to play in supporting the development of writing and other language skills. As curriculum training materials explain, 'The language of grammar offers clarity and economy. . . . Talking about patterns and features of language helps pupils become more aware of them and so to use them better as tools for thinking and expression'.[11]

But 'becom[ing] more aware' of language is regarded as desirable for other reasons too. There is a general commitment within the national curriculum to promoting *language awareness*, the ability to reflect consciously on the workings of language and so develop a more active or critical understanding of what is being accomplished through particular uses of it—in other people's speech and writing as well as one's own. Thus the key stage 3 requirements state that 'pupils should be taught to draw on their knowledge of grammar and language variation to develop their understanding of texts'—a requirement that seems most directly relevant to the study of literature and media (it could be fulfilled by activities such as examining the techniques of verbal persuasion used in advertising, working out the principles on which newspaper headlines or rap lyrics are constructed, or analysing the strategies used by novelists and poets to produce effects like suspense and irony). This is a broader view than the EPPI-Centre's of what linguistic knowledge is useful for: it encourages the integration of that knowledge into all the elements of English as a curriculum subject, not just the teaching of writing.

The approach to grammar that fits best with this view is a descriptive approach, one which focuses on the workings of real language in use. Yet while the overarching framework for dealing with language in the national curriculum is indeed descriptive, it is not wholly coherent or consistent: it has elements of prescription as well as description. To explain this, we have to recognize that the construction of a statutory national school curriculum is never a purely academic or technical exercise: it is an intensely political process. In the 1980s when the national curriculum for England and Wales was under construction, grammar was one of the issues on which opinion was most polarized, and the arguments most politicized. There was a three-way conflict between those who wanted the restoration of traditional prescriptive grammar-teaching, those who supported grammar but wanted a descriptive approach, and those who opposed the return of grammar in any form. As with any political struggle, the end result was something of a compromise. There were winners and losers (the descriptivists were the main winners and those who did not want grammar at all the main losers), but the final outcome had to be seen to make some accommodation to the key concerns of all parties.

One of the key concerns of the prescriptive camp was to embed in the school curriculum a particular view of standard English, as the common language of the whole nation which every child should use in both speech and writing. Both the other main camps disagreed: they were not against standard English as such, but they did take issue with the prescriptive camp's absolutist belief in its superiority to other dialects in all contexts and for all purposes. The way the national curriculum deals with the standard English issue reflects this history of argument about it. In some documents, references to the importance of standard English appear so frequently as to suggest an obsession with it. The key stage 3 speaking and listening requirements, for example, contain three separate statements saying that pupils should be taught to 'use standard English fluently in different contexts', to 'use the vocabulary, structures and grammar of spoken standard English fluently and accurately in informal and formal situations', and to understand 'the importance of standard English as the language of public communication'. Even if you do not disagree, you might wonder why the point needs to be made three times in as many pages. (One answer might be, to reassure the prescriptive absolutists that they won this battle even if they lost the larger war.)

But the prescriptivists were not the only constituency whose sensitivities had to be respected. Consequently, although the curriculum prescribes standard English, it avoids couching that prescription in overtly judgemental language. Rather than suggesting that the standard dialect must be used because it is 'good English' or 'correct English', documents stress that it is the most 'appropriate' form of English. As many commentators have pointed out, though, this is linguistic sleight of hand: it presents what is fundamentally a prescription (do A, not B) as if it were a neutral factual description (A is appropriate, B is not). The question that is elided here is why some kinds of English are more 'appropriate' than others, and who deems them to be so.

Perhaps, after all, the distinction between descriptive and prescriptive approaches to language is not as clear-cut as my earlier discussion suggested. When you describe some way of using language as 'appropriate', that may be an accurate description of the relevant facts, but it nevertheless has covert prescriptive force ('if you want to be appropriate, you should . . .'). Elsewhere I have argued that this blurring of the descriptive/prescriptive or fact/value boundary is difficult to avoid in relation to language, because language-using is fundamentally a social practice: some of the patterns we observe in actual usage arise from language-users' sensitivity to social norms and value judgements.[12] With any statement about language, it is always worth looking for the judgements behind the facts, and asking whose judgements they are, what criteria they are based on and whose interests they ultimately serve.

The national curriculum is not a seamless and monolithic document: it has been influenced throughout its existence by the conflicts around grammar and language which we have been considering throughout this chapter, and those conflicts have left their mark on it. Yet it could be argued that precisely because it is not a monolith, the national curriculum leaves scope for teachers to develop their own agendas, and to translate those into imaginative teaching. Questions that appear to be foreclosed in one set of requirements may be opened up again by another: for instance, the assertion of standard English's pre-eminence as 'the language of public communication' is immediately complicated by any encounter with the work of those critically acclaimed poets and novelists who do not regard standard English as appropriate for their purposes.

But for English teachers, exploiting the potential of the national curriculum and making it their own is a challenge, which not infrequently they feel ill-equipped to meet because of their own lack of experience studying language. To make the curriculum work for them and their pupils, rather than the other way around, teachers need to be able to think creatively about the various ways in which its requirements can be met; and to do that, they need to be confident in their own understanding of the subject. That is where I hope the following chapters can make a useful contribution.

Words

In AA Milne's *Winnie-the-Pooh*, Pooh at one point sings: 'Cottleston, Cottleston, Cottleston Pie/A fly can't bird, but a bird can fly'. This illustrates something that even very young children (and bears of very little brain) know about language: that there are different kinds or *classes* of words, which behave in different ways grammatically. 'Bird', for instance, belongs to the class of nouns; 'fly' can be either a noun ('winged insect') or a verb ('travel through the air'). Thus in English it is possible to say that a bird can fly, or that a fly can fly, but not that a fly can bird. This chapter will explore what users of English know about different classes of words.

Defining word classes

Traditional grammarians gave **notional definitions** of what they called 'the parts of speech' (i.e. **word classes**): formulas like 'a noun is a naming word', 'a verb is a doing word', 'an adjective is a describing word'. Definitions like these try to specify the general 'notions' which are basic to the meaning of any noun, verb or adjective. In practice, though, if you are trying to decide which class a particular word belongs to, these traditional definitions will often be less than helpful. For instance, you might reason that 'locomotion' and 'genocide' are verbs on the grounds that they are 'doing words', denoting actions rather than objects; but in fact both words are nouns. Equally, it might seem counter-intuitive to think of common verbs like 'be' and 'seem' as 'doing words', since 'doing' is not part of their meaning ('What are those people over there doing?' 'Oh, they're just seeming'). The statement that adjectives are 'describing words' is particularly unhelpful, since one might well think that describing is at some level the function of most words. (I still cherish the memory of a 'Fat Slags' strip in *Viz Comic* where a teacher tells Sandra she cannot propose 'cock' as an example of an adjective because it 'doesn't describe anything'. To which Sandra replies, with unassailable logic: 'it describes a cock, dunnit?')

This is one area where old habits die hard. Commercial revision guides for pupils taking SATs still emphasize the holy trinity of naming, doing and describing words, and it is also firmly lodged in the minds of many trainee teachers. The researchers Wasyl Cajkler and Jane Hislam asked some PGCE students to do a word-classifying task and at the same time to explain what they were doing by giving a 'think aloud' running commentary. Their comments revealed both their reliance on traditional definitions and the problems they encountered as a result. For instance, asked about the noun 'breath' in *take a deep breath*, one of the trainees said: '. . . some kind of doing . . . you take a breath . . . a doing word'. Another, considering the adverb 'softly' in *I landed softly*, said: 'Adjective—now I know it's an adverb (*-ly*), but an adjective because it's describing . . . I don't really know why . . .'[1] The trainees were doing their best to apply the notional definitions, but the result was that they assigned many words to the wrong classes, and were often not confident about their answers.

Notional definitions of word classes will always cause this uncertainty: their vagueness does not help, but the deeper problem is the idea that a word's grammatical class can be deduced directly from what it means. In fact, these are two different (and only tenuously related) things. Every word has its own meaning, but the class it belongs to depends on certain formal characteristics which it shares with other words: things like what endings you can or cannot add to it, and what positions it can or cannot occupy in the structure of a sentence. If we focus on form rather than meaning, the business of assigning words to classes becomes a lot less difficult, and the logic of the classification a lot less obscure.

Using formal criteria

The ability to classify words (which we all do automatically when we use them) does not depend on knowing what they mean. Sometimes, in fact, the reverse is true: our ability to classify an unfamiliar word helps us to guess its meaning in context, or at least to narrow down the possibilities.

Below I reproduce a case in point: the first stanza of Lewis Carroll's poem *Jabberwocky,* which contains a high proportion of nonsense words (shown here underlined). No one can say definitively what these invented words mean, but it is likely you will still be able to make an informed guess as to whether they are nouns, verbs or adjectives (take a moment to try this for yourself: in some cases you may think two answers are equally plausible.)

> Twas <u>brillig</u>, and the <u>slithy toves</u>
> Did <u>gyre</u> and <u>gimble</u> in the <u>wabe</u>
> All <u>mimsy</u> were the <u>borogroves</u>
> And the <u>mome raths outgrabe</u>.

My guess is that you classified the bold-type words as follows: 'brillig': either adjective or noun; 'slithy': adjective; 'toves': noun; 'gyre', 'gimble': verbs; 'wabe': noun; 'mimsy': adjective; 'borogroves': noun; 'mome': adjective or maybe noun; 'raths': noun; 'outgrabe': verb. The interesting question is how you came to these conclusions.

The answer is that you did it by using your tacit knowledge about the two main components of grammar: **morphology** (the form and internal structure of words) and **syntax** (sentence structure—roughly, the order the words come in). You classified the words by looking both at their structure (especially their grammatical endings) and at their position relative to other words. At this point I want to reconstruct the reasoning you must have used. If you find the reconstruction somewhat condensed and hard to follow, don't worry, because all the points will be revisited later. The point here is to reveal how much morphology and syntax you already tacitly know.

Let's begin with 'slithy toves', which I am betting you identified as an adjective + noun sequence. One reason for thinking 'toves' is a noun is the *-s* on the end of it: this ending indicates the plural, and in English plural endings only go on nouns. That is a morphological observation, about the internal structure of the word 'toves': that it consists of two units, a **stem** (*tove*) and an **affix** (*-s*). (Affixes are things you add or 'fix' to a stem, and they can be classified more specifically according to whether they are added to the beginning of the stem [*prefixes*] or the end [*suffixes*]). The presence of *-s* does not prove conclusively that 'toves' is a noun, though, because that ending does not just mark plurals: it also marks the third person singular of present tense verbs (e.g. *she works*). How do we know that 'toves' is the plural form of a noun rather than the third person singular form of a verb?

The answer is, because of the syntactic structure of the larger unit 'toves' occurs in. 'The slithy toves' on its own could be analysed syntactically in two ways: either as a sequence like *the lizard moves*, with 'slithy' being a noun and 'toves' a verb; or else as a sequence like *the slimy snakes*, with 'slithy' being an adjective and 'toves' a noun. Why is the second possibility more plausible? Once again, there is some relevant information in the form of the word 'slithy'. Its -*y* ending is found on a lot of adjectives (e.g. *slimy, shifty, shiny, sticky, prickly, tricky*). And if 'slithy' is an adjective then 'toves' has to be a noun, not a verb. We do not get sequences consisting of *the + adjective + verb*, like *the blue eats, or **the sure was fighting* (the asterisk before these examples is a linguist's convention meaning 'this is not a possible sequence in English'). By contrast, we do often get sequences consisting of *the + adjective + noun* (*the blue guitar*, *a sure thing*). But if we are not convinced, a look at the next line should convince us. The full context for 'slithy toves' is: 'the slithy toves/did gyre and gimble in the wabe'. 'Gyre and gimble' are readily identified as verbs, because they follow the **auxiliary verb** 'did', which is being used here to mark the past tense (normally it would be *the slithy toves gyred and gimbled*, but the 'did' option has been selected to make the line scan). Only verbs can have past tenses, so 'did gyre and [did] gimble' must be verbs. But that means that whatever comes just before 'did gyre and gimble' cannot be a verb, it must be a phrase built around a noun (telling us who or what 'did gyre and gimble'—in this case, 'the slithy toves').

The same principles allow us to classify the other nonsense words. 'Borogroves' and 'wabe' are clearly nouns, because they are preceded by 'the', which does not go before verbs (*the argued). 'Mimsy' looks like an adjective for the same reason as 'slithy', and also because it follows 'all'. 'All' is one of a set of words (others include *very, quite*) which only come before adjectives and adverbs. 'Brillig', coming after 'twas', could be an adjective, giving 'twas brillig' a structure like *it was warm*; but it could just as well be a noun (*it was dawn*), and we do not really have enough evidence to decide one way or the other.

'The mome raths outgrabe' is a bit trickier. If 'raths' is a (plural) noun then either 'mome' is an adjective (cf *the blue raths*) or else 'mome raths' is one of those compound terms made out of two nouns, like *history teacher*. Either way, if 'raths' is a noun then 'outgrabe' has to be a verb in order to complete the sentence. The alternative is to treat 'raths' as the verb, in which case 'mome' is a noun; but that leaves 'outgrabe' unaccounted for, and also means that the stanza has suddenly switched from past tense ('**did** gyre and gimble', '**were** the borogroves') to present tense ('the mome **raths**'). 'Outgrabe' could be like *gave*, a past tense formed by altering the vowel rather than adding *-ed*.

Even though you might not be able to explain how you did it, the fact is that to classify the nonsense words you must have used all the knowledge about English grammar that I have just presented in my reconstruction. That intuitive knowledge underpins all your efforts to extract meaning from language. Even when you *do* know what the words mean, you cannot decode what the text means without also mentally analysing the structural relationships between the words. And when you do *not* know what the words mean, it is still possible to extract some meaning from the text by analysing its grammar. *Jabberwocky* is nonsense verse, but it is not meaningless: Carroll understood that if he gave readers enough information to impose a grammatical structure on it, that structure would guide them to some kind of imaginative interpretation of the nonsense words and thus the whole poem.

Open and closed classes

What, though, does it mean to give readers enough information to impose a grammatical structure? One thing it means is that the words cannot all be nonsense. Carroll's nonsense words all belong to three classes: noun, verb and adjective. He does not tinker at all with the 'little words', items like *the, and, in, did,* for if these were also nonsense it would become impossible to identify his made-up nouns, verbs and adjectives. With a phrase like 'in the wabe', for instance, we can identify 'wabe' as a noun largely because of the preceding 'in the'.

There is an important difference between word classes like noun, verb and adjective, and the classes to which 'in' and 'the' belong. Nouns, verbs, adjectives and adverbs are **open classes**, so-called because it is always possible to add new members to them. New nouns, verbs, and adjectives are constantly entering the language (recent examples include the noun 'chav', the verb 'to text' ['send a text message to'], and the adjective 'nang' ['good']). But other word classes are *closed*: they contain a finite number of items and it is very rare for a new one to be added. Personal **pronouns** are an example of a **closed class**: the class contains the items. *I, you, he, she, it, we, they, one* and their variants (like *mine, your, him, herself, us, their, one's*). Another closed class is prepositions, words such as *of, with, by, on, at, around, about, in, out, up, down, to, from, before, after, behind, beneath*, etc. This class is quite large, but once again, the scope for adding to it is limited. (Incidentally, the distinction which I am making using the labels open class and closed class is sometimes made using the terms *content words* and *function words* or *grammatical words*.)

Word classes and their characteristics

The table below gives an overview of the main English word classes, with examples. (Note, however, that the table is not quite complete: I will be introducing one or two more closed classes later in the book.)

Table 1

Word class	Open/closed	Examples
Noun (N)	Open	*House, petrol, sincerity, Jane, globalization, quidditch*
(Main) verb (V)	Open	*Live, fill, seem, kick, globalize, text* (= 'send text message')
Adjective (Adj)	Open	*White, cheap, disgusting, global, phat*
Adverb (Adv)	Open	*Near, cheaply, globally, soon*
Preposition (Prep)	Closed	*With, from, of, down, up, in*
Pronoun (Pro)	Closed	*You, me, her, our, themselves*
Determiner (Det)	Closed	*A(n), the, this, that, these, those, some, any, many, no*
Auxiliary verb (Aux)	Closed	*Have, be, do*
Modal auxiliary verb (Mod)	Closed	*Can, could, may, might, must, will, would, shall, should*
Degree modifier (Deg)	Closed	*Very, quite, rather*

The next question is how we can tell which of these classes any given word belongs to. It is exactly the same question we addressed with the nonsense words in *Jabberwocky*, and the answer is that each class of words has its own distinctive characteristics, both morphological (what forms the word can come in) and syntactic (what positions the word can occupy in a sentence). Let us look at those characteristics in a more structured way.

The forms of a word: inflectional affixes

If we are trying to assign a word to its class, one of the most important characteristics to consider is its ability to take certain **inflections**, and its inability to take others. Inflections are (mostly) affixes—in English they are usually endings—which mark grammatical distinctions such as tense (past and present), **number** (singular and plural), possession, and so on. The same word can come in several differently inflected forms: for instance, *helps, helped* and *helping* are all forms of the word 'help', and would all be listed in the dictionary entry for 'help' rather than each getting their own separate entry. But which inflectional affixes you can put on a word (and which you cannot) will depend on what class it belongs to, so trying out the possibilities is a good test for word class.

The table below shows what inflectional affixes can typically be attached to words in the open classes: noun, verb and adjective.

Table 2

Word class	Typical inflectional affixes	Examples
Noun	-s marking the plural	*Cats*
	-s marking the possessive	*Cat's, cats'*
Main verb	-s marking third person singular present tense	*(It) seems, (she) fights*
	-ed (or vowel change) marking past tense	*Seemed, fought*
	-ing marking progressive	*Seeming, fighting*
Adjective	-er (or more) marking comparative	*Clearer, more horrible*
	-est (or most) marking superlative	*Clearest, most horrible*

If a word is a noun, it should be possible to put the plural affix -s and/or the possessive affix -'s on it. If a word is a verb, it should be possible to put the third person singular present affix -s on it, to inflect it for tense by either adding an -ed affix or changing the vowel (as with the verb 'fight' which becomes *fought*), and to add -ing to the end of it. If a word is an adjective, it should be possible to make it **comparative** or **superlative** by either adding the affixes -er and -est, as in *clear*, *clearer*, *clearest* or preceding it with the words 'more' and 'most', as in *horrible*, *more horrible*, *most horrible*.

The affixes which work for one class will not generally work for others. The word 'cat', for instance, can become *cats* (plural) or *cat's* (possessive), but not *cated, *cating, *cater or *catest. It takes the inflections nouns take, but not the ones verbs or adjectives take. The word 'seem' can become *seems, seemed* or *seeming*—you can add all the verb inflections—but not *seem's, *seemer or *seamest. The adjective 'shiny' can become *shinier* or *shiniest*, but not *shinies, *shiny's, *shinied or *shinying.

Some questions may have occurred to you while reading this. What about nouns that do not form their plurals by adding -s, but have an irregular ending (e.g. *children, oxen*) or no ending (*fish, sheep*), or are simply not words that occur in the plural (e.g. *furniture, photosynthesis, London*)? What about highly **irregular verbs** like 'be' and 'go' whose past tense forms (*was/were, went*) look completely unrelated, and adjectives like 'good' with its irregular comparative and superlative forms *better* and *best*? It is true that English is not fully regular, and that not all members of a word class will pass all the tests for that class. But we can still assess the balance of the evidence. For instance, 'child' may not take the plural -s, but it does have a plural form, it does take the possessive affix -'s, and it fails all the tests for verbs and adjectives (no *childed, *childing, *childer or *childest). It is therefore, on balance, a noun. Irregular though the verb 'be' is, it will pass at least one verb inflection test (you can add -ing to it), it has distinct (albeit irregular) third person singular present and past tense forms (*is* and *was*), and it fails all the inflection tests for nouns and adjectives.

Other questions that may have occurred to you are 'what about adverbs'? and 'what about closed class words?' With adverbs, inflectional affix tests will distinguish them from nouns and verbs, but they will not distinguish them clearly from adjectives (which is also a so-far unmentioned problem with using inflection tests to identify adjectives). Consider the adverb I have just used, 'clearly'. Like an adjective, it has a comparative and a superlative form (*more clearly, most clearly*). Some adverbs, like 'soon', can add -*er* and -*est* affixes. One feature that is often used as a rough diagnostic for adverbs is the fact that a large number of them end in -*ly*. (This is because one way to make an adverb is to take an adjective and add -*ly* to it, as in *clear—clearly*.) But this is not foolproof, since some adverbs do not end in -*ly* (e.g. *soon*), and some adjectives do end in -*ly* (e.g. *lonely, sickly, motherly*). To be certain of distinguishing an adjective from an adverb, we have to use the *positional* tests discussed in the next section.

In the case of closed class words, different classes behave differently. Some classes consist of fixed forms which cannot be inflected: prepositions, determiners and **degree modifiers**, for example. Another uninflected class is the **modal auxiliary verbs** (*can, could, will, would, shall, should, may, might, must*): in this case it is the lack of inflection which is the interesting thing about them, since it is the feature which distinguishes them from all other verbs. If we take 'must' as an example, there is no third person singular form *she musts, no past tense *musted* and no *musting*. (Auxiliary verbs which are not modals inflect in the same way as open-class main verbs: what differentiates them is, once again, their position in larger units.) Personal pronouns, on the other hand, do have inflected forms. Not only do they have possessive forms, as nouns do, many of them have different subject and object forms (the terms *subject* and *object* are explained in chapter 4: for now I will just point out that 'I', 'he', 'she', 'we' and 'they' are subject forms while 'me', 'him', 'her', 'us' and 'them' are the corresponding object forms). Personal pronouns also have **reflexive** forms ending in -*self* or -*selves*.

The order of words: positions in sentences

The basic insight of syntax, the study of sentence structure, is that words cannot just be put together in any old order. String them together at random and you will get what linguists call 'word salad', jumbled and unintelligible sequences like *where the is for jug*. As the linguist Noam

Chomsky once famously pointed out, there is a difference between saying that a sentence is 'meaningless' or 'nonsensical' and saying that it is 'ungrammatical'. He gave the example *Colourless green ideas sleep furiously*, noting that although this sentence does not make much sense, it is perfectly grammatical: it conforms to the rules for putting English words in order. Word salad, by contrast, is meaningless because it is ungrammatical, i.e. does not conform to those rules.

Knowledge about which words go with which and in what order is useful for working out what class a word belongs to. Each class has particular positions which it typically occupies relative to the other classes. Once again I will begin by giving an overview of these in a table.

Table 3

Word class	Typical positions	Examples
Noun	After a determiner	*The cat, those cats*
	After an adjective (or more than one adjective)	*Big cats*
		Colourless green ideas
Main verb	After an auxiliary verb	*Have seen, were going*
	After a modal auxiliary verb	*Might read, should help*
	After the infinitive marker 'to'	*To read, to help*
Auxiliary verb	Before a main verb	*Has fallen, is reading*
	After a modal auxiliary and before a main verb	*May have fallen, could be reading*
Modal auxiliary verb	Before any other verb, either Aux or V	*Might fall, may have fallen, could be reading*
Adjective	In the slot 'a ___ N'	*A small child*
	In the slot 'the N was ___'	*The child was small*
	After a degree modifier	*Very small, quite small*
Adverb	Before an adjective	*Unpleasantly sticky*
	After a verb	*See clearly*
	After a degree modifier	*Quite horribly, very nicely*
Preposition	Before a noun phrase (e.g. N, det N, det Adj N)	*In France, in the bathroom, in a pretty pickle*
Determiner	Before a noun or adjective + noun sequence	*Some people, some nice people*
Degree modifier	Before an adjective	*Quite small*
	Before an adverb	*Very unfortunately*

If a word is a noun, you should be able to put a determiner, an adjective or both before it. With verbs, the main issue is the ordering of the different types. If you only have a main verb in a sentence (e.g. *we **arrived** yesterday*, inflectional tests will be sufficient to identify it. But if you also have auxiliaries and/or modal auxiliaries, you can distinguish these from the main verb and from each other by looking at how they are ordered. Auxiliaries come before main verbs (*we **had** arrived the day before*) and modal auxiliaries come before both (*we **should** have arrived even earlier*).

In the previous section we saw that adjectives and adverbs can be hard to tell apart using inflectional criteria. In the table above we see that they also have one typical position in common: both can follow degree modifiers like 'very' (whereas nouns and verbs cannot: you do not get *very cat or *very fought*). The crucial difference between them, however, is that the two slots most likely to be occupied by adjectives— *the (adjective) noun* and *the noun was (adjective)*—cannot be occupied by adverbs. We can talk about *a clear sky* but not **a clearly sky*; we can say *the answer was clear* but not **the answer was clearly*. In the previous section I noted that some adjectives, like 'lonely' and 'sickly', end in *-ly*. We know these are adjectives, not adverbs, however, because they go in adjective slots: *the lonely goatherd*, *that wedding-cake was sickly*. If they were adverbs, these sequences would be ungrammatical (cf **the unfortunately goatherd*, **that wedding cake was horribly*.)

Another difference between adjectives and adverbs is that adverbs are freer to move around a sentence. For instance, all of the following are possible English sentences:

> The answer was clearly unwelcome
> Clearly the answer was unwelcome
> The answer, clearly, was unwelcome
> The answer was unwelcome, clearly

Move an adjective like 'unwelcome' around, however, and the results are rather different:

> The answer was unwelcome
> Unwelcome the answer was
> The answer unwelcome was

None of these sentences is word salad, but I can only imagine encountering the last two in either very bad verse, or the dialogue of a fictional character who is meant to be from another time or planet, like Yoda in the *Star Wars* films.

At the end of the chapter there is a complete list of formal tests for membership of the open English word classes. (We don't really need tests for the closed classes because they only contain a limited number of items, which are therefore immediately recognizable.) I have also provided some questions you can use for practice.

Word class, form and function

One issue that often comes up in relation to word class is whether the class of a word changes depending on its function in a particular context. For instance, given sentences like the following

> He dresses like a **geography** teacher
> Subscribers may borrow up to four **library** books
> The Queen hosts regular **garden** parties at Buckingham Palace

people often get into difficulties about whether 'geography', 'library' and 'garden' retain their normal status as nouns or whether they have turned into adjectives, 'describing' the following nouns 'teacher', 'books' and 'parties'. The answer is that they are still nouns, and the evidence is that they pass the formal tests for nouns, whereas the only adjective test they pass is being able to go in the slot *the __ noun*. Applying the other adjective tests results in ungrammatical sequences, as we can see if we compare sentences containing our test words with parallel examples which do contain adjectives (the adjectives are underlined):

> He dresses like the **nerdiest** teacher you've ever met
> *He dresses like the geographyest [most geography] teacher
>   you've ever met
> Subscribers may borrow up to four completely **new** books
> *Subscribers may borrow up to four completely library books
> The Queen's party was **sensational**
> *The Queen's party was garden

But if the words are not adjectives, what are they doing occupying the adjectival slot before a noun? The answer is that this slot is not reserved exclusively for adjectives. Nouns can also be *premodified* (*modifying* is the technical term for what traditional grammar calls 'describing') by other nouns. I will elaborate on that point, and explore its relevance for the teaching of writing, in chapter 5.

Another issue is raised by the sentence the trainee teachers in Cajker and Hislam's study were presented with:

> I take a deep breath and make a jump in the dark, I land softly near the door, tiptoe along the landing and have a wee.

Because of their dependence on the 'doing word' definition, many trainees identified 'jump' and 'wee' as verbs, though in this sentence they are nouns: both follow the determiner 'a', and in principle they could also be made possessive or plural, and be preceded by adjectives, e.g. *It took three big jumps to reach the landing*, or *I was disgusted by the wee's smell*. But if you put the same words into a different sentence, like *he was jumping up and down because he needed to wee*, formal tests show that they are in fact verbs ('jump' has the verb inflection *-ing* and is preceded by the auxiliary verb 'was', while 'wee' follows the infinitive marker 'to'). So are they nouns or verbs—or is it all a matter of context?

The solution is that 'jump' and 'wee' belong to a (fairly large) set of English words which can be both nouns and verbs. There are, in effect, two 'jumps' and two 'wees': the verb, and a noun which has been *derived* from the verb. Some writers call this acquisition of dual word-class membership *functional shift*; others call it **zero conversion**, because the word is converted from one class to another without any change in its base form. But in context, we can still tell which class the word is in by using formal tests. (Out of context, those tests will reveal that the word belongs to more than one class.)

The numerous English words that end in *-ing* require particularly close scrutiny, because the 'original' verb form is readily converted into a noun or an adjective. Consider

> She is **worrying** about next week's test
> Her constant **worrying** drives everyone mad
> The situation has become more **worrying** recently

In the first of these examples, positional tests tell us that 'worrying' is a verb (an inflected form of the verb 'to worry'). In the second example, however, 'worrying' is behaving like a noun, with the adjective 'constant' before it (note for collectors of terminology: traditional grammar labelled this kind of noun ending in -*ing* a **gerund**: the term is from Latin grammar, and is sometimes glossed as meaning 'verbal noun'). In the third example, 'worrying' is an adjective: it is comparative, 'more worrying', and it occupies an adjective slot (*the noun is ___*).

Zero conversion is not the only strategy for making new words in English. Words can also be converted from one class to another by adding affixes to them (add -*y* to 'sleep' and you get the adjective 'sleepy'; add -*ly* to that adjective and you get an adverb, 'sleepily'). This illustrates another sense in which words can have internal structure: we have already seen that they can be combinations of a stem and an inflectional affix, but they can also be combinations of a stem and one or more affixes that carry other kinds of meaning (e.g. 'educationalist' breaks down into *educate* + *tion* + *al* + *ist*). Morphology, the branch of grammar that deals with word structure, is concerned both with inflections and with the processes that enable us to form complex words like 'educationalist'. Since knowledge about it can be helpful in developing learners' vocabulary, reading comprehension and even spelling, in the next chapter we will take a closer look at English morphology.

Formal tests for open word classes

If a word belongs to a certain class, it will pass several of the tests for that class—though not necessarily all of them. Some tests will leave you with more than one possibility (e.g. it might be either N or Adj, Adj or Adv); in that case, you apply more tests for each possible class to see which has more 'passes' and fewer 'fails'. Class assignment is about which tests a word fails as well as which it passes.

Tests for nouns
Can you put a plural -*s* (or some other plural affix) on the end of it?
Can you make it possessive by adding apostrophe + *s*?
Can you put a determiner before it?
Can you put an adjective before it?

Tests for main verbs

Can you put a past tense ending like -ed on it (or otherwise inflect it for tense)?

Can you put the **progressive** ending -ing on it?

Can you put a third person singular -s on it?

Can you put a modal or other auxiliary verb before it?

Can you put the infinitive marker 'to' before it?

Tests for adjectives

Can you make it comparative/superlative (by adding -er/-est or 'more'/'most')?

Can you put a degree modifier like 'very' before it?

Can it go in the frame the ___ N?

Can it go in the frame the N was ___?

Tests for adverbs

Can you make it comparative/superlative?

Can it follow a degree modifier?

Does it end in -ly?

Can it go before an adjective?

Can it go after a verb, e.g. she said, ____

Can you move it to other positions in the sentence?

Some practice examples

Identify the class of the underlined words. In the case of open class words, use formal tests to give reasons for your identification. This is as much a test of your reasoning about grammar as it is a test of your ability to get the classification 'right'. In some cases there is more than one reasonable answer.[2]

> <u>Teaching</u> is <u>fun</u>
> It was a <u>shot</u> in <u>the dark</u>
> <u>He</u> <u>recycled</u> 300 <u>beer</u> <u>bottles</u>
> That top <u>would</u> go <u>brilliantly</u> <u>with</u> <u>your</u> blue skirt

3 | Morphology

In 2006 there was controversy about a film called *Kidulthood*, a grim portrayal of teenage life in west London which some people thought over-sensationalized. No one, however, seemed to have trouble with its title. Though 'kidulthood' was a novel, made-up word, people did not stand around their local multiplexes scratching their heads and inquiring of each other: 'what on earth is a "kidulthood"?'

'Kidulthood', like many words, can be broken down into smaller components of structure and meaning. If you understand these components, you will be able to work out what a new word constructed from them means. The -*hood* part of 'kidulthood', for instance, is an *affix* which is found on a whole series of words, or more exactly, nouns: you add it to a noun to produce a more abstract noun that means roughly, 'the state of being a [noun]'. Thus 'motherhood' is 'the state of being a mother'. -*Hood* has the same meaning when added to *father*, *brother*, *sister*, *wife*, *widow*, *bachelor*, *spinster*, *girl*, *boy*, *man*, *woman*, *baby*, *child*, *adult* and *parent* (though the word 'neighbourhood' is an exception, denoting a place). 'Kidulthood', then, is readily understood to mean 'the state of being a kidult'. But what is a kidult?

'Kidult' is obviously related to the words 'adult' and 'kid'. In fact, it is what is technically known as a **blend**, made not by taking two words and simply sticking them together (that would be a **compound**—the word 'whiteboard' is an example) but by joining the first part of one word to the last part of the other. There are a number of words like this in English, and often the blending reflects some kind of hybridity in the object or concept denoted. 'Brunch', a blend of 'breakfast' and 'lunch', denotes a meal intermediate between the two. A 'tankini' is an item of swimwear consisting of a tank top and a bikini bottom. 'Kidult', analogously, must mean 'person intermediate between a child and an adult'.

People sometimes complain that grammar stifles creativity, emphasizing conformity to rules at the expense of expressiveness, inventiveness or playfulness. But words like 'kidulthood' show how grammar in fact supports linguistic creativity. Without the structure grammar provides, novel uses of language would not communicate anything; if there were no rules, we could not produce meaningful effects by breaking or bending them. 'Kidulthood' is both structured and creative: it takes structural principles that are already recognizable to English-speakers and uses them to create something new. In this chapter I will look more closely at the way that process works—and why it matters for English teaching.

Morphemes, inflections and word formation

In chapter 2 I explained that *morphology* is one subdivision of grammar; the other is *syntax*, the study of sentence structure. I explained this in the context of a discussion of word classes, because one important indicator of a word's class is its ability to take certain inflectional affixes. Inflected forms of words have an internal structure: they can be broken into a *stem* and an inflectional affix. The plural noun 'cats' can be analysed as *cat + s*. The past tense verb 'borrowed' can be analysed as *borrow + ed*. The superlative adjective 'coolest' can be analysed as *cool + est*. We know that the inflectional affixes *-s*, *-ed* and *-est* are not themselves words: they cannot appear on their own, but only affixed to words of the appropriate class. We also know, however, that you can put them on any word of that class and they will always carry the same grammatical information (e.g. plural, past tense): so even if they are not words, they are clearly units of both form and meaning in the language.

'Stem' and 'affix' are perfectly good terms for *cool* and *-est*. But there is a more generic term for what I have just called 'units of form and meaning': the term **morpheme**. The *-eme* part of 'morpheme' means, roughly, 'smallest meaningful unit of'. A **phoneme** is the smallest meaningful unit of sound in a language; a morpheme is the smallest meaningful unit of grammatical form/meaning, with 'smallest' implying that it cannot be broken down into even smaller units. In many cases, the units we label morphemes are also words, like 'cool' for instance. You cannot break the form *cool* down any further. In other cases, though, a morpheme is smaller than a word—it is something that can be a component part of many different words, like the inflectional affix -*est*, which marks the superlative on many adjectives. Hence the word 'coolest' consists of two morphemes, *cool* and -*est*, one of which (*cool*) could stand on its own as a word, while the other could not.

But it is not only inflected forms of words that may consist of more than one morpheme. If we try to think of as many words as we can that contain the morpheme *cool*, the list will contain not only the inflected forms *cooler* and *coolest*, but also *coolness* ('the quality of being cool'), *uncool* ('not cool'), *coolant* ('liquid used for cooling an engine'), *coolbox* ('portable insulated container for keeping things cool'), and *coolhunter* ('person whose job is to detect emerging street trends and fashions'). Like 'coolest', these other *cool* words can be split into more than one morpheme, e.g. *cool + ness*. We know -*ness* is a morpheme, a unit in the language, because, like -*est* or the plural -*s*, it can be affixed to other words (e.g. *goodness*, *sadness*, *happiness*, *prettiness*, *unpleasantness*, *meanness*, *nastiness*, *sliminess*) and carry the same meaning as it does in 'coolness', namely 'the quality of being . . .'. But unlike superlative -*est* or the plural -*s*, -*ness* is not an inflection. Its function is not to mark grammatical distinctions such as number, person, case or tense, but to **derive** one kind of word from another: more exactly, to derive nouns from adjectives. The morpheme -*ness* is a resource for the process of **word formation**.

Inflectional morphemes are not resources for forming new words: nobody could claim to have formed a new word by simply adding -*s* to a noun or -*est* to an adjective. Nor do inflectional morphemes ever change the class of the word to which they are affixed. Morphemes that participate in word formation, however, can and often do change one class of word into another. The case of -*ness* is one example; another, which I mentioned at the end of chapter 2, is the way you can add -*y* to nouns to make adjectives, and -*ly* to adjectives to make adverbs, as in *sleep—sleepy—sleepily*. If adding an affix to something changes its word class, the affix is not inflectional, it is **derivational**.

Some of the *cool* words listed above exemplify another way of forming words: not by affixing but by *compounding*, putting together two words to create something which is more than the sum of its parts. For instance, the sentence *that's a cool box* does not mean the same as *that's a coolbox*. The compound 'coolbox' denotes a specific item, designed for the purpose of keeping things cool. Similarly, a 'blackbird' is a bird of a certain species, not just any black bird (female blackbirds are brown; ravens are black birds but not blackbirds). Compounds like 'coolbox' and 'blackbird' thus function as single words; but formally they can be split into two morphemes, each of which can also be used on its own, and each of which contributes something of its original meaning to the compound.

Morphology covers both the study of inflections and the study of word formation. In English, which is not a highly inflected language, there is more to know about the latter; and some of that has particular relevance for English teaching. Although word formation is an aspect of grammar, its educational importance has more to do with vocabulary. To succeed in school, learners need not only to extend their active vocabularies, but also to be able to make informed guesses about the meanings of unfamiliar words they encounter when reading. Many of these words are complex: to decode their meaning if you do not already know it, you have to break them down into their constituent parts—morphemes. Knowing something about morphology can help teachers to help learners develop strategies for doing that.

Making sense of English word formation

At first glance, what you see when you look at English is a seemingly limitless range of possibilities for making words. Consider, for instance, the range of affixes that can be used to make what we could broadly call abstract nouns. We have already looked at a set of terms that end in *-hood*, like *adulthood, parenthood*; but others end in *-ship*, as in *friendship, comradeship, leadership, partnership*. Many abstract nouns end in *-ness* (e.g. *goodness, niceness, sadness, happiness, nastiness, cheapness, unpleasantness*), but there are others that end in *-ity* (*necessity, futility, creativity, ability*), *-ment* (*movement, punishment, establishment*) or *-tion* (*action, corruption, direction*). When an English speaker makes a new abstract noun (whether it is new to the language or just new to them), how do they choose which of these affixes to form it with? Are there principles determining when it should be *-hood* or *-ship, -ness, -ment, -ity* or *-tion*?

There is no single infallible rule, but it is possible to say something about what differentiates these various noun-forming affixes. One significant factor is the word class of the stem to which an affix is being added. For example, as I pointed out earlier, words ending with -*hood* are nouns derived from other nouns (specifically, nouns denoting categories of person), and they mean 'the state or status of being [noun]'. -*Ness* words on the other hand are derived from adjectives, and mean, 'the quality of being [adjective]'. This does not work for all cases (e.g. 'warm' and 'hot' become *warmth* and *heat*, not *warmness* and *hotness*; 'relevant' becomes *relevance* and 'indignant', *indignation*), but it does work for a large number. The -*ment* and -*tion* words listed above, by contrast, are derived from verbs ('move', 'punish', 'establish', 'act', 'corrupt', 'direct'), and these nouns generally mean 'the act or process of [verbing]'. If a word belongs to more than one class, it will be possible to derive more than one kind of abstract noun from it. 'Correct' can be both a verb and an adjective: sure enough, we have both 'correction' ('the act/process of correcting'), derived from the verb, and 'correctness' ('the quality of being correct'), derived from the adjective. So English speakers making decisions about how to derive an abstract noun from an existing word will be influenced by their knowledge that the class of the existing word conditions both the choice of affix and the meaning of the resulting noun. (If an abstract noun is ever made from the word 'chav', it will be *chavhood* or *chav[i]ness,* not *chavity* or *chavment*.)

Another factor that can influence speakers' choices is whether the stem is a native Anglo-Saxon word or a word that was borrowed into English from another language—the most important foreign sources being French and Latin. For instance, the -*ity* words listed above are borrowed from Latin. Words with -*ment* in most cases come from French, while -*tion* words also tend to have origins in either French or Latin (French being itself a direct descendant of Latin). The influence of French also underlies the tendency for an adjective ending in -*ent* or -*ant* to be converted into a noun ending in -*ce*, or -*cy* (rather than, say, -*ness*), which is seen in *fragrant—fragrance, important—importance, decadent— decadence, current—currency*. This way of forming nouns from adjectives is common in French, and words that behave similarly in English generally entered the language from French. In the process of borrowing words from other languages, English incorporated some of the strategies which were used to form words in those languages.

Of course I am not suggesting that present-day English speakers have this historical knowledge stored in their heads. Although the pattern whereby *-ant* adjectives become *-ance* nouns rather than *-ness* nouns is objectively a product of the historical influence of French, contemporary speakers who reproduce that pattern are more likely to be acting on another principle which affects word formation (and linguistic behaviour more generally): the principle of *analogy*. For instance, if a speaker knows a series of (fairly common) adjective-noun pairs that follow the same pattern, like *different/difference* and *important/importance*, s/he can apply that knowledge to analogous but less common cases, converting, say, 'defiant' to *defiance* (and not *defiantness*) even if s/he has never encountered the word 'defiance' before. This propensity to analogize is something that can be drawn on in the classroom, in activities like trying to think of as many words as possible that have the same ending, like *-ness* or *-ance* or *-tion,* and then considering what they have in common; or trying to form as many words as possible with different endings from a recently coined (perhaps slang) word that as yet has few established derivatives; or focusing on a group of related words and asking where and why there are deviations from the normal pattern (for instance, why do we have *manly, womanly, fatherly* and *motherly* but not *childly*—and why *brotherly, sisterly, wifely* and *daughterly* but not *husbandly* or *sonly?*).

More ways of forming words

Forming nouns of the kind we have been looking at is just one of the many possible uses of derivational morphemes in English. Here I cannot list all the possibilities, let alone examine them all in detail. To give you some sense of the bigger picture, though, here is a table showing some of the ways words of one class can be derived from another using affixes (this of course omits the derivational processes which only involve a single class, like making *-hood* and *-ship* nouns from other nouns). You will probably be able to think of many additional possibilities:

Table 1

To make a . . .	Into a . . .	Possible affixes	Some examples
Noun	Verb	zero (no affix)	*phone, text, email, light, fish, picture, paint*
		-ify	*glorify, versify*
		-ize	*sermonize, soliloquize*
Noun	Adjective	*-y*	*slimy*
		-ish	*childish*
		-ful	*faithful*
		-al	*logical, global*
		-(i)ous	*pompous, vicious*
Verb	Noun	zero	*sleep, work, help*
		-ment, -tion ('act or process of verbing')	*punishment, correction, construction*
		-er/-or ('agent who verbs')	*skater, killer, singer, actor*
		-ation	*imagination, globalization*
Verb	Adjective	*-able/-ible*	*readable, convertible*
		-ing	*disgusting*
		-ive	*creative, repulsive*
Adjective	Noun	*-ness*	*sadness, happiness*
		-ance/-ence	*fragrance, salience*
		-ity	*pomposity, futility, senility*
Adjective	Verb	*-ize*	*rationalize, globalize*
		-en	*redden, gladden*
Adjective	Adverb	*-ly*	*happily, globally*

All the affixes in this table are word endings; but of course, English words can also be formed using *prefixes*, affixes added to the beginning of a word. The *pre-* of 'prefix' is an example: we also find it with the same meaning ('before') in words like *premature, predispose, premonition*. A number of morphemes which negate or invert the meaning of whatever follows are prefixes, like *un-, in-, dis-, mis-* and the *de-* in *decompose, devalue* and those terms so beloved of lifestyle gurus, *detox* and *declutter*. Some prepositions are commonly prefixed to words to make other words: 'over', for instance, is found in *overcome, overtake* and *overlook* (which do not mean the same as 'come over', 'take over' and 'look over'); 'out' occurs in *outbreak*, *outrage*, *outcome* and *outwit*; 'up' and 'down' contribute to *uplift*, *upscale*, *uptake*, *downcast*, *downsize* and *downtrodden*. (You will notice that the pattern here is for prepositions to be combined with verbs, though the resulting word is not always a verb—*outbreak* and *outcome* are nouns, while *downtrodden* is an adjective, with no verb 'to downtread'.)

Morphology and register

Some quite common prefixes in English (e.g. the *inter-* of 'international', the *multi-* of 'multicultural' and the *super-* of 'supermarket'), as well as many of the suffixes (endings) in the table above, are borrowed from Latin. So, in fact, are a large proportion of the words that appear in the more formal **registers** of English. Although it is something of an oversimplification, there is some truth in the idea that native English or 'Anglo-Saxon' words are the plain, earthy ones, while words borrowed from French are fancier, and Latinate words more formal. (If you were presenting awards to people who had done something brave at a formal ceremony you would not praise the recipients for their 'guts' (English) but would be more likely to refer to their 'courage' (French) or 'fortitude' (Latin)). This means that there is a gap between the vocabulary of everyday and formal registers in English—a gap that has to be bridged as part of the process of becoming educated.

The concentration of Latin-derived terms in formal English is in large part the product of a process—part of the longer process of language standardization—that occurred during the 16th and 17th centuries. In histories of English it is usually called '**elaboration**' or 'enrichment'. To make English usable in domains of activity where previously either French or Latin had dominated, such as education and scholarship, law, administration and religion, there was a need to extend its vocabulary so that the relevant matters could be discussed in an appropriately formal register. This need was addressed by borrowing large numbers of terms from Latin, the language educated people had been schooled in. However, there were people who objected to the resulting influx of Latinate words, dubbing them 'inkhorn terms'. The words were criticized mainly for being difficult to understand; but some people also disliked them because they were foreign imports: if new words were needed, the critics thought they should be made from native Anglo-Saxon materials. Had these people won the argument, we would now be visiting the *bookhoard* rather than the *library*, and complaining about the *darkness* rather than the *obscurity* of new words. Possibly, there would be less of a gap between the everyday vocabulary of English and its formal registers. But the anti-inkhorns did not win the argument, and the register gap is a real issue. Reading is the activity which makes the most important contribution to extending vocabulary, but reading itself becomes frustrating if you are constantly confronted with words you cannot make sense of. That is one argument for looking in a structured way at some of the Latin-derived morphological units which are common in formal written English.

Morphology and spelling

Another area of English teaching in which some knowledge of morphology (both inflectional and derivational) may be useful is spelling. As everyone knows only too well, English spelling is not a matter of simple one-to-one correspondences between sounds and letters. A great deal of effort goes into teaching children systematically how the more complex relationship between sound and spelling actually does work in English. But even the best-designed *phonics*-based approaches overlook an important point about English spelling: that it is systematically influenced by morphological as well as phonological factors. In some cases our spelling system represents the structural features of a word rather than the way it sounds—morphology trumps *phonology*.

One case in point is the spelling of inflectional affixes like those that mark plural, possessive and (regular) past tense. We can use the plural as an illustration here. In spoken English, there are three forms of the plural affix. One is the sound /s/, as in *cats*; another is /z/, as in *dogs*; and some words add a syllable, /ɪz/, as in *horses*. Which of these forms is used depends on the characteristics of the last sound in the stem. If the last sound is s, z, sh, or ch, it is pluralized by adding /ɪz/. Otherwise, if it is a *voiceless*[1] consonant like p, t, or k you add /s/, and if it is either a *voiced* consonant like b, d, g, m, n or else a vowel, you add /z/. The behaviour of English speakers from a very early age shows that they know this rule: they apply it consistently, to newly encountered or made-up words as well as familiar ones (try it for yourself on *kronge*, *funip* and *blid*). But when children learn to write, they must learn to disregard the phonetically conditioned variation in plural endings and spell all of them the same way: <s>.[2] Essentially, the spelling principle is to represent the grammatical abstraction (plural) rather than the way any particular variant of it sounds. Exactly the same thing happens with possessives (all <'s>, though the spoken form varies in just the same way as plural *-s*), and with past tense *-ed*, a spelling that again encompasses all three spoken variants, /t/ (as in *coughed*), /d/ (as in *sneezed*) and /ɪd/ (as in *snorted*).

If you ask a literate adult how to make a plural or a past tense, they will tell you the spelling rule: 'add *-s*; add *-ed*'. Unless they have studied linguistics they will probably not be able to state the rules for spoken English (even though they follow them consistently when they speak): they may have no conscious awareness that there is more than one plural or past tense ending in speech. When literate people think about language, they invariably use the written form as their mental template, so what is obvious to them is the spelling rule. But teachers need to realize that for learners acquiring literacy, this rule is not obvious. If a teacher does not recognize that the written plural *-s* or past tense *-ed* is an abstract representation of a grammatical unit which in speech has three different forms, she may fail to spot the non-random errors in a child's spelling which suggest that the child has not grasped that point either.

There are other cases in which a spelling problem can be sorted out using morphological, not phonic, principles. For instance, some learners have trouble with the difference in spelling between *-tion* words and words ending *-cian* (e.g. *magician*, *musician*): the two affixes sound exactly the same, making for errors like **magition*. What needs to be explained here is that if the word means 'someone who is an expert in something' or 'someone who does something as their job' it will end in *-(c)ian* (cf *magician*, *musician*, *technician*, *logician*, *physician*, *mathematician*, *beautician*, *mortician*, *librarian*); if it does not have that meaning then it will be a *-tion* word.

The examples I have just given come from the work of Terezinha Nunes and her associates, whose research has led them to argue that children benefit significantly if literacy teaching pays attention to morphological as well as phonological patterns. (Both their results and some of the classroom materials they have developed can be accessed online.[3]) For teachers, morphological knowledge is also useful for the purpose of analysing and assessing certain aspects of writing.

Looking at pupils' writing

As I noted in chapter 1, it is important to make a systematic assessment both of what learners can do and of what they cannot yet do, in order to judge what kind of intervention might be called for at any given stage. With that in mind, let us consider the passage below, which is an extract from a narrative by Hosman, a Year 8 EAL (English as an **additional language**) pupil, about a school trip in Colombia.

> I was walking in a line up a hill it was very hard to walk up the hill Becaas there was a lot of graval to walk up. One of the boy's trip me up and fell down and cut my slef and the boy kep on going walking I cry from the cut that I got on my knee and one of one of the village pepole help me up and the man had a donkye and was dress all in wiht and had a hat. He had a long roBp that had the colomBian flag. he put a plaster on my knee and He put me on top of his Donkey.

An impressionistic examination of this text suggests that Hosman has a problem with tense: the narrative time-frame seems to shift between past and present, and some verbs are not inflected for tense at all (e.g. *one of the boys trip me up*, which has neither the past tense *-ed* nor the present tense *-s*). However, this is a very general and in some ways misleading assessment. On closer examination there is a non-random pattern about which verbs have overt past tense marking and which do not:

Table 2

Verbs marked for past tense	Verbs not marked for past tense	Verbs that could be either
Was, fell, got, had, put	Trip, cry, help, dress	Cut [same form in both tenses], kep [not clear if this is *keep* or *kept*]

The verbs which appear marked for past tense are all *irregular verbs*, where the past tense is *not* formed by adding -*ed*. By contrast, the verbs which appear unmarked for past tense are all **regular verbs** where the past tense *is* formed by adding -*ed*. Three of the four are also cases where the spoken form of the past tense morpheme would be pronounced /t/. One of the ambiguous cases, *kep*, is interesting in this connection: the past tense of 'keep' is formed *both* by changing the vowel (like *fall/fell*) *and* by adding an ending, which in this case is spelled as it sounds, /t/. Hosman gets the vowel change but not the ending.

All this suggests that Hosman's problem is not with tense in general but specifically with the regular past tense morpheme -*ed*. Studies of both first and **second language** acquisition in English show that common irregular past tense forms usually emerge before the regular form. The lag may be because irregular forms are learnt as separate words, whereas the regular forms follow a general grammatical rule, and that takes more time to work out. In addition, the regular past tense is not easy to hear when people speak at a normal speed and volume. Final consonants, especially /t/, are often weakened (replaced with glottal stops or otherwise 'swallowed'): they stand out much less clearly than the vowel sounds which distinguish pairs like *fall* and *fell*. In any case, the fact that Hosman does mark tense consistently on irregular verbs suggests he already knows about the relationship of tense to time and the need to keep tense consistent in a narrative. What he still needs to learn is that most English verbs form past tenses with -*ed*, and that this ending has to be overtly marked in writing.

For practice: dividing words into morphemes

What you are looking for when you try to divide words into their component morphemes is separable chunks which (a) can either stand alone or be combined with other morphemes to make other words, and which (b) retain the same combination of form and meaning whatever word you make them part of. With both these points in mind, try splitting the following words into their component morphemes. For each morpheme you identify which is not a word in its own right, justify your decision to count it as a morpheme by (a) giving examples of other

words in which the same unit can be found, and (b) giving some account
of the meaning or the function of the unit. (My own analyses and
comments can be found in the notes to this chapter.[4])

Anticlockwise; *internationalism*; *parliamentary*; *kidulthood*; *vilification*;
scandal; *disadvantageous*; *slimeball*; *supercalifragilisticexpialidocious*.

Sentences

4

In this chapter we move from morphology to *syntax*, the structure
of sentences, and in particular, the grammatical constituents that make
up sentences. I will look more closely at some of these in the next few
chapters: this chapter is about establishing the bigger picture before we
go on to fill in the details. A good place to begin is with the question:
what *is* a sentence?

One popular definition, often found in traditional grammar books, is:
'a complete thought expressed in words'. Let me express in words some
of my own thoughts about this.

> Thanks a lot
> Good grief!
> Really?

Though my thoughts are complete, traditional grammarians would not
consider my verbal formulations of them to be 'proper' sentences. Like
the notional definitions of word classes we considered in chapter 2,
the 'complete thought' definition of a sentence misses the point that
grammatical units, though important for meaning, are fundamentally
units of linguistic *form* or *structure*.

Another popular definition of a sentence is 'what comes between a
capital letter and a full stop'. So long as we assume that sentences only
exist in writing (and add a sub-clause to cover those that end with ?
and !), this definition is watertight—but it does not explain how anyone
knows where to put the capital letter and the full stop. This makes it
especially useless for educational purposes, since where to begin and end
sentences is one of the most difficult problems confronting learners when
they begin to write (and often for quite a long time afterwards). There

are no capital letters or full stops in speech: the job of breaking the
continuous flow into meaningful and manageable chunks is mainly done
by using the resources of **prosody** (pitch, stress, loudness, tempo). To
many inexperienced writers it is far from self-evident how to translate the
primarily prosodic structure of speech into the syntactic structure of writing.

Here for instance is the opening of one learner's written narrative
about breaking his arm (I have edited out spelling errors for readability):

> My first time I broke my arm because I was riding a bike
> and my brother got in the way of the bike so my arm
> went on the wheel and my dad took me to my nan's to
> get a car to the hospital and my brothers went to see my
> mum in the pub and I went to the hospital with my dad
> and I sleep in the hospital for 6 weeks and I went home
> and the next day I went to school and I did not write or
> do no work I play on the computer in the classroom.

This text replicates in writing the typical structure of a spoken narrative:
it is a series of statements about events, sequenced more or less in order
of their occurrence, and joined together by 'and'. Inserting more full
stops to mark sentence boundaries would be a rather arbitrary process,
since there are various places where they could go, and in many cases
no particular reason to insert them at one point rather than another.

Yet there are definitely places where they could *not* go, or to put it
another way, stretches of text which English-speakers would not regard
as possible sentences. If you were given the task of breaking the text into
sentences, you would not do it like this:

> And my brother got in the way of the bike so my arm. Went on the
> wheel. And my dad took me to my nan's to get. A car to the hospital
> and my brothers went to see. My mum in the pub.

You would probably do it like this:

> And my brother got in the way of the bike. So my arm went on the
> wheel. And my dad took me to my nan's to get a car to the hospital.
> And my brothers went to see my mum in the pub.

In the second version, the strings of words which come between the capital letters and the full stops are all grammatical, i.e. possible rather than impossible, sentences. In the first, by contrast, they are not: many of them seem to have a piece missing.

> And my brother got in the way of the bike so my arm. *So my arm what?*
> Went on the wheel. *What went on the wheel?*
> And my dad took me to my nan's to get. *To get what?*

Perhaps this is what the 'complete thought' definition of a sentence is really driving at: the idea that we have intuitions about when a sequence of words is complete and when there is something missing from it. However, what these intuitions are about is not primarily the completeness of the *thought*. To see what I am getting at, consider the examples below:

> Rained again yesterday
> Might be fine weather later

In spoken English these would be acceptable sequences, if perhaps a tad brusque, but in writing you would want to complete them by putting something at the beginning of each:

> <u>It</u> rained again yesterday
> <u>There</u> might be fine weather later

Yet it would be difficult to argue that the addition of 'it' or 'there' makes the thought expressed in each sentence any more complete, since it adds no information at all. The 'it' in *it rained* is not like the 'it' in *pick it up*, where 'it' is a pronoun standing for some previously mentioned entity. You could ask 'pick <u>what</u> up?', but no one would ever ask, '<u>what</u> rained?' Our feeling that 'it' or 'there' are missing from certain sequences of words, and would need to be added to make those sequences acceptable in writing, is not a feeling about meaning, it is a feeling about sentence *structure*. We know that there are certain structural slots in a sentence, which have to be filled for it to be a complete sentence—even if what they are filled with has no content, but is just a 'dummy' placeholder like the 'it' in *it rained*.

Sentence constituents: subject, verb and object

The main structural slots in a sentence contain what are known as the *subject*, the *verb* and the *object*. I should immediately qualify that by saying that not all sentences have objects: as I will explain below, that depends on what the verb is. But in English, almost all sentences (the exceptions are **imperative** sentences like *Walk, don't run!*) need something to fill the subject slot and the verb slot. That is why we need the 'it' in *it rained*: because otherwise we would have only a verb and no subject. Here are some sentences consisting of a subject plus a verb:

Table 1

Subject	Verb
Life	sucks
Her mobile phone	rang
My sister	is visiting
The old man	has died
Pigs	might fly

You will notice that what fills each of these slots is not necessarily a single word, though it can be. The grammatical slots in a sentence are for *phrases*, units which can consist of one or more words. Phrases are built around a word of a particular class (so if they are only one word long, that word will be from the class in question). The verb slot, unsurprisingly, is filled by a main verb, which may or may not be accompanied by modal and other auxiliary verbs (in *life sucks* we have only a main verb; in *pigs might fly* we have a main verb and a modal). The subject slot is filled by a *noun phrase*, a phrase which either consists of a noun (e.g. 'pigs' in *pigs might fly*) or is built around a noun (e.g. *her mobile **phone***), or else is a pronoun. This last possibility may seem puzzling, since in chapter 2 we considered pronouns as a separate word class from nouns: what explains it is the fact that pronouns' grammatical function is *substituting* for noun phrases (e.g. ***it*** *sucks*, ***she*** *is visiting*, ***they*** *might fly*). Pronouns therefore often appear—on their own—in the slots which are prototypically filled by noun phrases. (Chapter 5 has more to say about noun phrases.)

In English **declarative** sentences (those which are statements, not questions or commands), it is usual for the subject to come before the verb. If there is an object in the sentence, it will usually come after the verb. The normal constituent order in English, then, is *subject + verb + object*, or in shorthand, SVO. This is a common order in the languages of the world, but not the only possible one: Welsh, for instance, has VSO and Hindi and Urdu have SOV. Specifying a 'normal' order does not mean that other orders are impossible, but it does imply that they will be understood as deviating from the norm for a reason. In poetry, for instance, departures from the normal order may be used to make a line scan and/or fit the poet's rhyme scheme (e.g. *'where the bee sucks, there suck I/In a cowslip's bell I lie'*). In conversation a constituent that would normally go last may be put first in order to emphasize it (e.g. *that one I really like*).

Whether a sentence has an object depends on what the verb is. With some verbs objects are obligatory, with others they are optional, and there are also verbs which do not permit them. Like the subject slot, the object slot is generally filled by a noun phrase. Here are some examples:

Table 2

Subject	Verb	Object
I	am making	a pie
Some supermodels	earn	millions of dollars
You	have solved	the mystery
My sister	is visiting	her in-laws
Elephants	might fly	jumbo jets
The deadline	expired	_____

The first three examples are cases where the verb needs an object: without the object the sentence would feel incomplete (e.g. *I am making*). Then there are two sentences, *my sister is visiting her in-laws* and *elephants might fly jumbo jets* where the sentence would not feel incomplete if you removed the object: these verbs can be either **transitive** (taking an object) or **intransitive** (not taking an object). Finally, 'the deadline expired' is an example in which the verb cannot have an object.

Other constituents

Here you may be thinking, 'but all kinds of things could go after 'expired': what about 'yesterday' or 'in 1965?' And indeed, you could add these to the sentence, but they would not be objects: rather they would fill an optional slot known as the **adverbial** (or in some approaches to grammar, the *adjunct*). The easiest way to see that this is a different slot from object is to look at some examples where both slots are filled:

Table 3

Subject	Verb	Object	Adverbial
I	am making	a pie	for dinner
You	have solved	the mystery	already
My sister	visits	her in-laws	very frequently

The adverbial constituents are both less essential (these sentences would still be structurally complete without them) and less restricted in their position than subjects, verbs and objects: in each of these examples it would be possible to move what is in the adverbial slot to the beginning of the sentence (e.g. *for dinner I am making a pie*). Another difference concerns what can fill the adverbial slot. One possibility is to put an *adverbial phrase* like *very frequently* in it; another is to fill it with a *prepositional phrase,* i.e. a phrase that begins with a preposition such as 'for' or 'to'.

As we have already seen, not all verbs can be followed by objects. Sometimes, though, an intransitive verb will be followed by something that looks a bit like an object, in the sense that it appears in the same position, and may also be a noun phrase. Here are some examples:

Table 4

Subject	Verb	?
My mother	was	a teacher
That	seems	a reasonable idea
That idea	seems	reasonable
Jane	has become	an insufferable bore
Jane	has become	insufferable
I	am feeling	totally confused

The constituent in the slot I have labelled '?' is known as the **complement**. Complements typically follow verbs like *be*, *become*, *seem*, *appear* and (in some senses) *feel*, which do not denote actions the subject does to someone or something, but rather states of existence or transition which the subject experiences or is defined by. What goes in this slot can either be a noun phrase (e.g. *a reasonable idea*, where the key word is the noun 'idea'), or an adjective phrase (e.g. *totally confused*, where the key word is the adjective 'confused'). Either way, though, what appears in this slot will be further information about the subject. This means it is not an object, for objects and subjects are different entities.[1] To see this distinction, compare these two sentences:

Jane **has met** an insufferable bore
Jane **has become** an insufferable bore

In the first sentence we know that the bore is someone other than Jane. In the second, by contrast, we know that the bore *is* Jane.

In the course of this discussion it will probably have become apparent to you that the different constituents of a sentence contribute different elements of its meaning. Putting it a little more technically, there is a tendency for certain constituents to be associated with certain **semantic** roles (the term 'semantic' means 'to do with meaning'). Here it is useful to recall Paul Tench's observation which I quoted in chapter 1, that grammar categorizes experience in terms of 'happenings'—who did what to whom, when, where, how and why. Subjects, verbs and objects are connected to the 'who did what to whom' part of this (prototypically, subjects are the 'who' and objects the 'whom'); adverbials add information about 'when, where, how and why'. (Complements do not fit quite so well into Tench's scheme: the verbs that they follow are about being rather than doing, and that is reflected in the kind of meanings they contribute.)

However, English provides resources for the same information to be structured grammatically in more than one way. Being able to structure information in different ways in order to produce different effects is an important skill, especially for writers (since in writing you are generally more dependent on grammatical resources: speakers can also make use of prosody). To make it clearer what I mean, let us look in more detail at one of the grammatical choices English offers—and at why understanding the implications of that choice might be useful for learners' development both as writers and as critical readers.

Structure, meaning and focus

Let's start with the sentence *Mary hit John*. This is a stereotypical example of the 'who did what to whom' type of sentence, where the subject is associated with the role of **agent**, the person(s) responsible for the action denoted by the verb (in this case the one who hits), while the object is associated with the role of **patient** (the term is from the Latin word for 'suffer'): the recipient, target or victim of the action (in this case, the one who gets hit).

But users of English know that there is another way to express this set of meanings. 'Mary hit John' can be reformulated as 'John was hit by Mary'. The difference between the two versions is that the first is in the **active voice** and the second is in the **passive voice** (from now on I will just talk about active and passive sentences). Here are some more illustrations:

Table 5

Active sentence	Passive sentence
The teacher rewarded the girl	The girl was rewarded by the teacher
Big Brother is watching you	You are being watched by Big Brother
A dog ate my hamster	My hamster was eaten by a dog

The words 'active' and 'passive' are related to 'agent' and 'patient'. When you make an active sentence into a passive sentence (which you can only do if the verb has an object: you cannot for instance say *the old man was died*, because 'die' is an intransitive verb), what you do is take the noun phrase in the object slot and move it into the subject slot. This means that the original occupant of the subject slot, the agent, gets pushed out. You can either move it into a prepositional phrase following the verb and beginning with 'by', as in *John was hit by Mary*, or you can delete it altogether to produce *John was hit*. The latter is perfectly grammatical, since the two slots in a sentence that have to be filled, subject and verb, *are* filled: it is just that the subject slot now highlights the semantic role of the patient rather than the agent. The other difference between our active and passive sentences is the form of the verb: *hit* becomes *was hit* (to form any passive sentence, we use auxiliary 'be' plus the past **participle** form of the following verb). But what really makes the difference to the overall effect is the 'promotion' of the object to the subject slot.

Why do I call this a 'promotion' and what is the effect of it? The 'promotion' metaphor reflects the observation that whatever goes in the subject slot will tend to be understood as the topic or theme of a sentence. When you say *Mary hit John* you are constructing a sentence that highlights what Mary did. If instead you say *John was hit by Mary* you are changing the focus to highlight what was done to John. And if you delete the agent and just say *John was hit* you are focusing exclusively on what happened to John, since this formulation does not mention who hit him.

In certain *registers* (varieties of language used in particular contexts and institutions), passive sentences are very common, and **agent deletion** is frequent. Here are some examples: the question is what purpose(s) the use of the agent-deleted passive serves in each.

1. The solution was heated to a temperature of 100 degrees centigrade
2. PRESIDENT KENNEDY ASSASSINATED
3. The Bank of England is not expected to raise interest rates in the short term
4. Litter should be placed in the receptacle provided

Example (1) is scientific English: conventionally, the passive is used for reporting scientific experiments. The reasons usually given for this are (a) that it makes scientific writing more concise, and (b) that it conveys the impersonal and objective nature of scientific procedures and observations. Agents are usually deleted, since *who* performed the act of heating the solution (the writer, a lab assistant, etc.) is not important. Using a grammatical construction that allows you not to mention the agent avoids distracting the reader with scientifically irrelevant details, and saves space for more important information like the exact temperature to which the solution was heated. Some critics would argue, however, that the scientific passive is not just a neutral convention that reflects the impersonality and objectivity of science, but an ideologically motivated convention which helps to construct our belief in the impersonality and objectivity of science.

Example (2) is a headline, a brief, condensed summary of a news story. Here, the choice of the agent-deleted passive reflects 'news values', calculations made by journalists about what makes an event newsworthy. If someone shoots the President of the USA, then his status as a world leader—and of his death as a world event which will have far-reaching consequences—means that he, not the assassin, will be highlighted as the topic. Whether headlines about crime highlight the agent (criminal) or the patient (victim) will usually depend on their relative newsworthiness. If a serial killer who has featured in previous news reports commits another murder, we might expect headlines like *RIPPER STRIKES AGAIN*, because the killer is more newsworthy than any individual victim. However, if a crime victim is famous, powerful or particularly vulnerable (e.g. a young child), then victim-focused headlines like *TV STAR ATTACKED* or *GIRL, 7, MURDERED*, are more likely.

This last example is part of a real headline from *The Sun*, which in its full form read: *GIRL, 7, MURDERED WHILE MUM DRANK IN THE PUB*. As Kate Clark has pointed out, in this headline the deletion of the agent of 'murdered', combined with the added detail about where the victim's mother was when it happened, has a very particular implication: it invites readers by inference to blame the mother for the child's death, since she is the only person overtly mentioned as doing anything. Clark found that this was a repeated pattern in *The Sun*'s reporting of murder, rape and domestic violence. If in the newspaper's view a woman was not 'respectable', its headlines were constructed in such a way as to blame her, rather than the actual assailant, for crimes committed against her or her children. Where a victim was deemed to be 'respectable', by contrast, the headline usually highlighted, and often demonized, the perpetrator (e.g. *EVIL SEX FIEND MURDERS GIRL, 7*).[2]

In example (3)—which could come from a news report, policy document or academic article on economics or finance—the passive is probably being used for one or both of two reasons: to conceal or at least render vague who was the source of the information regarding

---

the Bank of England's intentions, or to present the writer's own opinion on the matter as if it represented some general consensus. In academic and bureaucratic registers, the agent-deleted passive often has the latter function: texts are littered with assertions that begin *it is thought/believed/expected/understood*. . . . Critical readers will always ask who exactly it is who thinks, believes, expects or understands, and whether the agentless passive formulation is an attempt to influence their perception of an issue by presenting a certain view of it as a generally accepted truth.

Example (4) is a public notice which contains two uses of the passive, both with agents deleted (*should be placed* and *provided*). This reflects the fact that it is addressed by an institution to a mass audience. If the agents had not been deleted it would read, redundantly and somewhat absurdly, *Litter should be placed by you in the receptacle provided by us*. (Or more explicitly and even more absurdly, *litter should be placed by members of the public in the receptacle provided by the council sanitation department*.) But why not just say, *Put your litter in the bin*? This is a matter of politeness: to avoid sounding offensively bossy or unnecessarily confrontational, notices are often written in maximally indirect, impersonal and formal language. This one uses ultra-formal vocabulary (e.g. 'placed' for 'put' and 'receptacle' for 'bin' or 'container') as well as passive syntax. The formality and impersonality of the passive mean that it is frequently found in public notices and announcements, even though it can make them ambiguous (like the much-ridiculed notice informing London Underground passengers that *Dogs must be carried on the escalator*).

In different contexts, then, deleting the agent in a sentence by choosing the passive rather than the active can serve different purposes. More generally, what you choose to put in which constituent slot will make a difference to the effect the sentence produces – what the recipient will take it to be about, and what s/he will understand you to be emphasizing. For instance, users of English will tend to identify the subject of a sentence as its theme or topic and the rest of the sentence as saying something about it. At the same time, putting something in the first, subject slot tends to imply that it is 'given' rather than 'new' information—something that the hearer or reader can be expected to be aware of, whether because it has already been mentioned explicitly or because it is part of shared background knowledge.

Once again, though, speakers and writers have some range of options for signalling what the topic is or highlighting important information. One strategy they can use is to *dislocate* a constituent from its normal position in the sentence and put it somewhere else. In speech we quite often find 'left **dislocation**', which means moving something which would not ordinarily come first, since it is not the grammatical subject, to the very beginning of an utterance (so to the left, if we visualize the words on a page), in order to identify it as the topic:

> <u>My mother-in-law</u>, I wouldn't say she was fat, but . . .
> <u>Trainspotting</u>, what's that about?
> <u>90 miles an hour</u> he was doing

It is also possible to dislocate rightwards to ensure that the most important new information goes *after* the verb. This is one motivation for using 'dummy' subjects like *it* and *there*. For instance, why have I chosen to use 'it' as my subject in the first sentence of this paragraph, *It is also possible to dislocate rightwards*? The alternative, *Dislocating rightwards is also possible*, is equally grammatical, and shorter; but it would put the new and important point at the beginning, thus presenting readers with information they are unprepared for and potentially sending the misleading message 'you know what I'm talking about already'. The message I want to send is, 'here comes some new information which I am going to expand on in the next bit of text'. Skilled writers continually keep track of what their readers already know or don't know, expect or do not expect, and structure information with that in mind.

Looking at pupils' writing

Below is an extract from a Year 10 pupil's writing in which he addresses the question 'Why has the James Bond movie genre continued to be successful over the past 40 years?' At whole text level, the information is organized by structuring the essay as a list of reasons for the popularity of James Bond films. What I want to look at is the structuring of information at *sentence* level, using the grammatical resources of constituent structure. What strategies does the writer use, and what effect do his choices have on the effectiveness and cohesiveness of the whole text?

> *At the start of the film a woman always appears. She is usually naked and dancing. I think that this convention has [been] successful for generations. This is because it keeps the audience more entertained, and it is something which they expect to see.*
>
> *In <u>Doctor No</u> they set scenes in exotic locations like the Caribbean. In the UK, they don't set high standards. They don't have things like the beautiful scenery and huge mansions as they do in the Caribbean.*
>
> *Another reason why James Bond has been successful is because the villains have been very interesting. . . . Villains usually have a fortress and also always do a race against time towards the end of the movie.*

In these three paragraphs the writer considers three factors which make James Bond films popular: naked women, exotic locations and interesting villains. In some places he shows skill in using sentence structure to establish topics and to highlight new/important information. For instance, in the third paragraph the subject of his opening sentence is *Another reason why James Bond has been successful*. This establishes the topic, and it contributes to textual cohesion by tying the new paragraph to preceding ones (<u>*Another*</u> *reason*). It also allows the writer to put the new information, that interesting villains are 'another reason', after the verb 'is'. In subsequent sentences, 'villains'—now established as 'given'—becomes the subject, and the rest of the sentence tells us something more about why James Bond villains are interesting.

The paragraph about exotic locations, however, is less successful in establishing clearly what the topic is and tying it into the overall text structure. One reason for this is that the writer makes the pronoun 'they' the grammatical subject of all his sentences. In the first place this raises an issue about who 'they' are. Pronouns are **deictic** terms (this term is from Greek and means 'pointing to'): to interpret them it is usually necessary to find some entity in the preceding text which the writer is using a pronoun to refer back to. In this case there has been a recent establishing the basic point that his father bought glasses, he tells us what the glasses cost, names their brand, and compares them to the glasses worn by a character in a film. The writer of sentence (2), by contrast, uses only simple NPs, which in most cases consist of just a noun with a determiner before it, like *the man*, *a donkey*, *a hat*. His strategy for building up his description of the man is to put each new detail into a separate sentence-like unit (*the man had a donkey*; [*the man*] *was dressed in white*; [*the man*] *had a hat*). If the first writer had used this technique, he might have written something like: *My Dad had bought some glasses. The glasses were Ray-Bans and they cost £50. They looked like the glasses Mr Jones has in* Men in Black 2. Clearly, the strategy he actually uses is more economical: condensing the information into a single noun phrase enables him to add detail without repeating himself or impeding the overall flow of the text.

This kind of condensation is a characteristic of skilled writing, but it is a skill learners have to develop rather than something they naturally know how to do. Condensing information in the manner of the first writer is essentially a literate strategy, whereas the approach of the second writer is closer to what we do naturally in spontaneous speech. At this point it may be helpful to examine that difference, and the reasons for it, in more detail.

Spoken and written language: the density of information

Here is a piece of informal spoken English, transcribed from a recording of conversation among friends. (The = indicates *latching*, where one speaker starts speaking immediately after another with no pause, and the square brackets show where speakers overlap each other):

A: And she didn't she didn't she didn't like Katy =
B: = no she didn't [like Katy
A: [she didn't like Katy at all

In spontaneous speech, speakers have little time to plan ahead and hearers are obliged to process what is said 'as it comes'. It helps both parties, therefore, if the information load is fairly low, and if the same information is given more than once. In the extract above, the speakers take three turns and 20 words to establish the proposition that 'she didn't like Katy at all'. Once you take out the false starts (*she didn't she didn't she didn't*) and the parts where one speaker just repeats the other's words (*she didn't like Katy/no she didn't like Katy*), there are actually only eight *different* words ('and', 'she', 'didn't', 'like', 'Katy', 'no', 'at', 'all'). The noun phrases are simple, consisting of the single words 'she' and 'Katy'.

Writers, by contrast, have more time to plan and edit, while readers have various processing options which are not available to hearers—if they cannot immediately extract all the information they can go back and read the text again. Readers have no need (and writers no excuse) for the repetitiveness that is so striking in the 'Katy' extract; on the other hand, readers do need all the information necessary for understanding to be provided explicitly in the text itself, since unlike hearers in conversation, they will not usually be able to ask the text's producer for clarification. These considerations make it both possible and desirable for written language to have a higher density of information than spontaneous speech. The density is most noticeable in the noun phrases, which tend to be much longer and more complex than the ones we typically find in informal spoken English.

Here for instance is a sentence of academic writing, with the noun phrases underlined:

> <u>This seminar</u> will take <u>the findings of the Nuffield Inquiry</u> and <u>the government's literacy strategy</u> as <u>a starting-point for the exploration of the current situation in language education in the UK</u>

This sentence is not only longer than any of the utterances in the 'Katy' conversation, it is also much more densely packed with information: of its 31 words, 25 are different, with only the closed-class words 'the', 'in' and 'of' used more than once. And virtually all this information is contained in the noun phrases, which among them account for all but three of the 31 words. The NP in the first, subject slot, 'this seminar', is not complex, but as we move to the right of the verb—the place in a sentence where new information is typically highlighted—the NPs get more elaborate, culminating in the 15-word monster at the end.

The following passage is from a different genre of writing: its source is Mark Haddon's novel *The Curious Incident of the Dog in the Night-time*. Once again, though, there is a concentration of detailed information in the noun phrases:

> I used **my special Maglite torch** and **a piece of mirror from the utility room** to help me see into **the dark spaces at the back of cupboards where the mice used to get in from the garden**

In the academic NP reproduced above, the writer's main purpose in adding detail is to specify the topic of the seminar with as much precision as possible (*the current situation in language education in the UK*). In Haddon's fictional text the detail is used for a more descriptive purpose, to help the reader visualize what the narrator is seeing. In this particular novel, that is important for characterization as well as plot: Haddon has created a narrator, Christopher, who tends to focus obsessively on details because he has Asperger's syndrome, a form of autism. Very detailed descriptions like the one quoted provide one way of showing the reader how someone like Christopher perceives the world.

It is interesting to note, though, that Haddon's technique for building up detailed descriptions does not involve using a lot of adjectives. In the long NP at the end of the passage there is only one adjective, 'dark'; in the whole passage there are only two, the other being 'special' in *my special Maglite torch*. Although adjectives are considered to be prototypical 'describing words', and some teachers encourage pupils to add them as a way of making their writing 'more descriptive', I hope this chapter will clarify that adjectives are only one resource, and not necessarily the most important one, which skilled writers use to make their descriptions more vivid or more precise. To see what other resources can be used for these purposes—and why exploiting them may often be preferable to just adding lots of adjectives—we need to take a closer look at the way English noun phrases are structured.

What noun phrases are made of: heads, premodifiers and postmodifiers

The core element in any phrase is the word which serves as its *head*—the word around which everything else in the phrase is organized. In a noun phrase this head word will be either a noun or a pronoun. Here are some illustrations: in each sentence there are two NPs (occupying the subject and object slots), and each head noun is underlined.

Table 1

Subject	Verb	Object
<u>She</u>	didn't like	<u>Katy</u>
The <u>man</u>	had	a <u>donkey</u>
<u>I</u>	used	my special <u>torch</u>
This <u>seminar</u>	will discuss	the government's literacy <u>strategy</u>

The first sentence, *She didn't like Katy*, illustrates the most minimal type of NP, one that contains only the head. The second sentence illustrates another simple NP structure in which the head is preceded by a determiner: 'man' is preceded by the definite article 'the' and 'donkey' by the indefinite article 'a'. In the last sentence we have a further example of the same structure, *this seminar*. The other NPs, however, *my special torch* and *the government's literacy strategy*, illustrate that determiners are not the only words you can put before a head noun. In *my special torch* the adjective 'special' comes before the head noun 'torch'; in *the government's literacy* strategy the noun 'literacy' comes before the head noun 'strategy'.

Adding information to an NP by inserting adjectives or nouns before the head noun in a noun phrase is technically known as premodification —in other words, the head noun is modified by something that comes before (*pre*) it. That 'something' can in fact be a whole list of **premodifiers**, as in the song lyric

She wore <u>an itsy-bitsy, teeny-weeny, yellow polka-dot bikini</u>

where everything between the determiner 'an' and the head noun 'bikini' is premodifying 'bikini'. Theoretically there is no limit on how many premodifiers you can put in this position: I could describe a bikini using even more of them than the song does:

> She wore <u>a hideous, ill-fitting, saggy, baggy, acid yellow, polka-dot bikini</u>

But this is not always the most effective strategy for building up a description. One problem with it is that too many modifiers coming before the head noun may cause the hearer or reader to lose track. It is not easy to follow a list of 17 adjectives describing something when you do not yet know what the thing in question is—you are waiting for the head noun to tell you. It is easier to assimilate this volume of detailed information if it comes after rather than before the noun which is being elaborated upon: in other words if the head is not premodified but **postmodified**.

If we go back to the noun phrases in the two pieces of text I reproduced earlier, the academic prose and the extract from a novel, we will see that many of them do favour postmodification, putting most of the information they contain after the head. For instance (the head nouns are underlined):

> the <u>findings</u> of the Nuffield Inquiry
> a <u>starting-point</u> for the exploration of the current situation in
>   language education in the UK
> the dark <u>spaces</u> at the back of cupboards where the mice used to get
>   in from the garden

It is possible, as the last of these examples demonstrates, to use both pre- and postmodification in the same NP. The noun 'spaces' here is premodified by the adjective 'dark', but the postmodification is more extensive, and that is not a coincidence. After the head noun is where the greatest potential exists for increasing the information density and the level of detail or precision, by making use of certain grammatical possibilities. In the next section we will look in more detail at what these possibilities are, and what they enable writers to do.

More on postmodification: recursive structures

Looking at a long and complex NP like *a starting-point for the exploration of the current situation in language education in the UK*, the thought may well have occurred to you: 'surely there is more than one noun phrase here'. Isn't 'the UK' a noun phrase, with the same, *determiner + noun* structure as 'the man' or 'a donkey'? Doesn't 'the current situation' have the same, *determiner + adjective + noun* structure as *my special torch*?

The short answer to these questions is yes: this long and complex noun phrase does contain other, shorter and less complex noun phrases. But 'contain' is the operative word here. To see what I am getting at, consider the following:

I need <u>milk</u>, <u>eggs</u>, <u>butter</u>, <u>self-raising flour</u>, <u>caster sugar</u> and <u>a pinch of salt</u>

Each of the underlined portions in this example is a separate noun phrase; the organization is that of a *list*, in which all the phrases are structurally on the same level. Grammatically it would make no difference if we changed the sequence of the items (e.g. to *self-raising flour, a pinch of salt, caster sugar, butter, eggs and milk*): because they are structurally on a par, these phrases can go in any order. But *a starting-point for the exploration of the current situation in language education in the UK* has a very different kind of organization: it is not a list in which every NP is on the same level as every other, but a *hierarchical* structure where there are NPs within NPs. The NP whose head is 'starting-point' (i.e. the whole thing), is like one of those painted Russian dolls you pull apart to reveal a slightly smaller doll, which in turn comes apart to reveal an even smaller one, and so on. The NPs lower down the hierarchy are constituent parts of the ones above, and the meaning depends on these vertical relationships. Unlike the items in the list of ingredients, whose relationship to each other is horizontal rather than vertical, the smaller NPs in the hierarchically organized phrase are not interchangeable: switching their order would produce nonsense (e.g. *the UK for a starting point of the current situation of the language education in the exploration*).

To see how the hierarchical, Russian doll structure is actually put together, let us look at a rather less complicated example, *the findings of the Nuffield Inquiry*. You will probably be able to pick out two NPs in this, 'the findings' and 'the Nuffield Inquiry', so I should start by asking how we know that at the highest level of structure the whole thing is one phrase, consisting of a smaller NP ('the Nuffield Inquiry') nested inside a larger one ('the findings of the Nuffield Inquiry'). Let's remind ourselves of the context in which the sequence we are considering appears:

Table 2

Subject	Verb	Object
This seminar	will take	the findings of the Nuffield Inquiry . . .

If we want to know whether something is a single noun phrase, there are two formal tests we can use. One is to try replacing our putative NP with a pronoun (pronouns always replace whole NPs, not just nouns, so if we can replace the whole thing with a pronoun that means the whole thing is one phrase); the other is to try moving our putative NP to some other position in the sentence (e.g. by making the sentence passive). If the whole thing really is a phrase, then once again, the whole of it will move.

In the case of the sentence we are looking at, these tests yield

This seminar	will take	them
The findings of the Nuffield Inquiry	will be taken	by this seminar

The fact that these are both grammatical sequences tells us that 'the findings of the Nuffield Inquiry' is indeed one NP. For the sake of completeness, though, let us investigate the alternative hypothesis, that 'the findings' and 'the Nuffield Inquiry' are two completely separate NPs, by trying to replace or move each of them separately. This disproves the hypothesis by producing almost entirely ungrammatical results:

*This seminar	will take	them of the Nuffield Inquiry
This seminar	will take	the findings of it
*The findings	will be taken	of the Nuffield Inquiry by this seminar
*The Nuffield Inquiry	will be taken	the findings of by this seminar

Formal tests confirm, then, that 'the findings of the Nuffield Inquiry' is a single noun phrase, which contains, Russian doll-style, 'the Nuffield Inquiry'. In fact, 'the Nuffield Inquiry' is one component of a phrase which is *intermediate* between itself and 'the findings of the Nuffield Inquiry': '**of** the Nuffield Inquiry', which is a *prepositional phrase* (PP). It consists of a preposition—'of', which is also the PP's head—plus the noun phrase 'the Nuffield Inquiry'.[1] The whole NP has the structure:

Table 3

Determiner	Noun	Prepositional phrase
The	findings	of the Nuffield Inquiry

Prepositional phrases are very commonly used to postmodify nouns. The NP structure shown above, *determiner + noun + prepositional phrase*, is also the structure of, for instance, *the wheels **on the bus**, a bridge **over troubled water**, the cat **in the hat**,* etc. And because a prepositional phrase can contain a noun phrase (which in turn may contain another prepositional phrase postmodifying its head) this is a structure you can recycle over and over to produce more and more levels of detail. For instance, in these examples I have added an extra prepositional phrase:

Table 4

	Det	N	Prepositional phrase
The findings of	the	Inquiry	into language education
The cat in	the	hat	with a tassel

And I could clearly go on in the same way. 'Into language education' could become *into language education **in Britain***; 'the hat with a tassel' could become *the hat with a tassel **on the end*** (and that could be further extended to *on the end **of it***).

If we now return to the very long NP from the academic seminar announcement—*a starting-point for the exploration of the current situation in language education in the UK*—we see that it follows exactly this recycling principle. Each head noun is postmodified by a prepositional phrase (e.g. *a starting-point <u>for the exploration</u>*), which contains another noun phrase ('the exploration'), whose head noun is postmodified by a prepositional phrase ('of the current situation'), and so on. This example calls it quits after four recyclings, but it would be possible to go on adding more: how about, *a starting point for the exploration of the current situation in language education in schools with large numbers of pupils from* bilingual *communities in major urban areas of the southeastern region of the UK*?

What I have just called 'recycling' is known more technically as **recursion**, and it is the property of human languages which explains our capacity to make, as Noam Chomsky once put it, 'infinite use of finite means'. A language has only so many words and so many ways of putting them together, but because these can be used *recursively*, we can go on building more and more complex structures, with no upper limit on how many levels we can add. Chomsky observed that because of this, a grammatical sentence in English can in theory be infinitely long—though in practice, of course, there will come a point when we run up against the limits of our memory, our ability to stay awake or our interlocutor's patience.

Some children's rhymes play with the property of recursion. An example is *The House that Jack Built*, which begins with the line 'This is the house that Jack built' and gradually adds to it to produce sequences like:

> This is the man all tattered and torn, that kissed the maiden all forlorn, that milked the cow with the crumpled horn, that tossed the dog that worried the cat that killed the rat that ate the malt that lay in the house that Jack built.

Here, once again, the same kind of sequence is being used recursively (it is recurring at each successive level) to make a noun phrase longer and longer. But in *The House that Jack Built* the sequence in question is not a prepositional phrase. Rather it is a **relative clause**, a sequence like *that Jack built* or *that ate the rat* which postmodifies a noun (e.g. *the <u>house</u>* [*that Jack built*], *the <u>cat</u>* [*that ate the rat*]).

Relative clauses (we will look in more detail at what a clause is in chapter 7) are constructions which allow a speaker or writer to insert what amounts to an extra sentence into a noun phrase. You could think of 'this is the house that Jack built' as the sum of two sentences:

'This is the house' + 'Jack built the house' = 'This is the house that Jack built'.

The sentence we end up with has the structure:

Table 5

Subject (NP)	Verb	Complement (NP)
This	is	the house that Jack built

You can test for yourself that 'the house that Jack built' is indeed a noun phrase, by using the pronoun replacement test. (The whole of it can be replaced with the pronoun 'it'; the smaller component parts cannot.) Here are some more sentences in which the NP to the right of the verb contains a relative clause postmodifying the head.

Table 6

			Head	Relative clause
This	is	the	cat	that ate the rat
This	is	the	cat	that someone rescued
This	is	the	present	a student gave me
This	is	the	spy	who loved me

Because they involve recursive structures, the postmodification strategies we have been looking at in this section are powerful tools for writing. Postmodifying a noun with prepositional phrases or relative clauses enables a writer to build internally complex structures which are densely packed with information. Using adjectives to premodify nouns, though it has its place in a writer's repertoire, does not offer the same scope for developing extended and highly organized descriptions. As this section has hinted, there is an important difference between organizing information in list-like structures (e.g. a list of NPs like *milk, eggs, butter and flour* or a list of adjectives like *an **endless clear blue shimmering** sea*), and organizing information hierarchically. In the next section I want to explore that difference, and its implications, a little further.

What complex noun phrases do

The piling up of complex, hierarchically structured noun phrases is a particularly striking characteristic of academic English, and it is especially prominent in scientific writing. The linguist Michael Halliday has argued that this is not just an unmotivated stylistic convention, but has functions which are relevant to the enterprise of creating and manipulating knowledge.[2]

Perhaps the most straightforward of these functions is increasing the amount of information packaged in a sentence. Each time you embed another NP you are adding more information—but you are doing it in a particular way. Just laying NPs end to end or *coordinating* them with 'and' results in a list, like the list of cake ingredients I gave earlier or the list of gifts in the song *On the First Day of Christmas* (*five gold rings, four calling birds, three French hens, two turtle doves and a partridge in a pear tree*). But if you embed the NPs in other NPs using recursive structures like the ones described above, you are not simply listing items, you are qualifying your description of a single item with more and more details (*a partridge in a pear tree from a game reserve in Wiltshire with a particular reputation for the quality of its partridges*). This is a key difference between a flat structure (the list) and a hierarchical, multi-levelled one. It is not hard to see how the latter might be useful for making the fine distinctions and giving the detailed definitions that are important in science (and other academic endeavours).

But Halliday also draws attention to a characteristic of certain nouns and noun phrases which we have not yet discussed. Let us go back to what might look like one of the simpler noun phrases we have encountered in this chapter: *the government's literacy strategy*. Actually this is more complex than it might look, for you could think of it as a grammatical re-packaging of two separate propositions:

> The government has a strategy
> The strategy relates to literacy

'The government has a strategy' becomes *the government's strategy*; 'the strategy relates to literacy' becomes *the literacy strategy*; the two are condensed into the single phrase *the government's literacy strategy*.

This kind of condensation is called a **nominalization**, a term which means 'the process/result of making something into a noun or noun phrase'. I say 'noun or noun phrase' because some nominalizations are single words rather than phrases like 'literacy strategy'. For example, in *the exploration of the current situation*, the word 'exploration' is in effect a condensation of the idea *someone explores something*—it is a whole proposition boiled down into one noun. Another example is 'findings' in *the findings of the Nuffield Inquiry*, which condenses the proposition *someone found something*. ('Nominalization', aptly, is a nominalization itself, as are many -*ation* and -*ing* nouns derived from verbs.)

Halliday studied the historical evolution of scientific writing in England from the 17th century onwards, and found that the use of nominalizations increased over time. Early scientists tended to write about experiments as events, using a quasi-narrative register to describe their actions and the processes they observed; but as they developed a modern understanding of science as a quest for general truths and invariant laws, their writing became more nominalized and less focused on events unfolding in time. When you condense a proposition into a noun or a noun phrase, you eliminate the verb that would be there if the proposition were expressed in a sentence. There is a link between using verbs and locating whatever you are describing in time: verbs are the carriers of tense, the grammatical expression of time. Since nouns do not have tense, nominalization has the effect of transforming what might be seen as timebound (specific, concrete, dynamic) events or processes into timeless (general, abstract and static) entities. Halliday calls this a *grammatical metaphor*, and suggests that it facilitates objectification, abstraction and generalization—all of which are important for the purposes of science.

Scientific and academic registers are not, however, the only ones that use nominalization extensively. Tabloid newspaper headlines are also famous for it. Here are two examples, with the nominalizations underlined.

SIGN SWITCH STUNT FOILED (*The Sun*, June 14 2006)
KIDS SEX TXTS ALERT (*Sunday Mirror*, June 11 2006)

Sign switch stunt foiled heralds the story of a speeding motorist who unsuccessfully tried to avoid a ticket by switching the 30 mph speed-limit sign he had just disobeyed with a nearby 40 mph sign. *Kids sex txts alert* reports that children have been receiving explicit sexual material via their mobile phones.

These tabloid headline nominalizations work in much the same way as academic ones like *literacy strategy*. *Kids sex txts alert*, for instance, condenses the information that the police have been **alerted** that children (**kids**) are receiving text (**txt**) messages of a **sex**ual nature. In headlines as in academic prose, nominalizations are useful for increasing the density of information—getting more content into fewer words (in the case of tabloid headlines, very few words). The timeless quality of phrases without verbs also serves a purpose in headlines, though not the same one it serves in science writing. Headlines are not usually intended to be statements of abstract truths: rather their lack of tensed verbs reflects the immediacy or 'nowness' of news. There are other differences too: tabloid headline nominalizations tend to be strings of short, common nouns rather than the Latinate abstractions of academic prose; alliteration (*sign switch stunt*) and assonance (*sex t(e)xts*) give the resulting phrases a playful quality which is generally absent from academic writing. In short, while both academic and tabloid headline registers of English use nominalization, you would not generally mistake one for the other.

Looking at pupils' writing

Here are two different pieces of writing (extracts from, respectively, a Year 8 pupil's scary story and the Year 10 pupil's discussion of James Bond films which we examined in the last chapter). The issue I want to consider is how the writers exploit the possibilities of noun phrases to convey information in a way that suits their purposes in writing.

> ### The scariest place I've been!!
> Well I'm not really a scary place person, but the most scariest place I've been is in my friend Naomi's house when we were watching a movie called <u>The Others</u>. I was laying down watching it when my friend's mum slammed the door and frightened us (she's wicked). The film had a very eerie feeling and the room felt as if it was full of ghosts.

> Why has the James Bond movie genre continued to be successful over the past forty years?
> (. . .) Extreme sports are another convention of the films. James Bond has been successful at doing extremely dangerous sports. He knows what he is doing and he is an expert at doing it. The audiences enjoy the excitement of watching these sports. It always ends in a thrilling sequence.
>   In most of the films the opening titles use a blend of sex and violence. In all of James Bond movies, the movie starts with naked women dancing and with guns and bullets and blood pouring down the screen.

The first text is a personal narrative whose writer has adopted what seems to be a deliberately informal, conversational tone, reflected in speech-like interpolations like the opening *well* and the parenthetical *she's wicked*, and also in the (informal but inventive) noun phrase *a scary place person*, where 'person' is premodified by the noun 'place' (which is itself premodified by the adjective 'scary'). In a more formal piece of writing the same idea might be communicated in a less condensed NP involving prepositional phrases and relative clauses— e.g. *the kind of person who likes scary places*. This writer clearly can use relative clauses: *the most scariest place I've been* contains one. Most of her NPs do not elaborate on the basic information they provide (e.g. *the room*, *the door*, *my friend's mum*), which is in keeping with the conversational tone, but it means that when she does choose to elaborate (e.g. *a very eerie feeling*), even though the adjective 'eerie' is conventional in scary stories, it stands out.

The James Bond text is more analytic, and the writer is evidently aiming for a higher level of formality. He is good at using 'of' prepositional phrases which allow him to pack information into his NPs and to maintain an academic tone: examples are *another convention of the films*, *the excitement of watching these sports*, *a blend of sex and violence*. 'Excitement' and 'blend' are nominalizations: expressing these concepts as nouns allows them to be incorporated into larger NPs and expanded on using postmodifiers, so the writer is showing skill in exploiting grammatical possibilities here.

Arguably, however, this piece is not a good advertisement for the idea that you make descriptions more effective by using adjectives (and adverbs premodifying adjectives), as this writer does in *extremely dangerous sports* and *a thrilling sequence*. In both cases the head nouns are generic terms ('sports', 'sequence'), and the addition of 'extremely dangerous' or 'thrilling' does little to make them more specific or precise (I can visualize *paragliding* or *white water rafting*, but *extremely dangerous sports* conjures up no particular image). For my money, the job the writer wants to do is done much better in the next paragraph, where he uses a series of single concrete nouns: *guns and bullets and blood*. The contrast between this and *extremely dangerous sports* underlines the point that putting adjectives before nouns is not a foolproof recipe for producing effective descriptions. What matters is, first of all, to choose the right nouns; and then to make judicious choices about whether and how to elaborate by constructing larger phrases around them.

Verbs

This chapter considers some of the things that can be done with verbs in English. Though verbs may carry less of the informational content of a text than the noun phrases we looked at in chapter 5, their grammatical role is pivotal: the verb in a sentence in effect determines many features of that sentence's overall make-up. For instance, it is often the form and placement of the verb that communicates whether a sentence is a statement, a question or a command. Whether or not the verb is transitive determines whether there will be a slot in the sentence for an object, and whether the sentence can be formulated in the passive voice. The verb is also the part of the sentence that locates whatever is being talked about in time.

This chapter does not try to cover everything about the way English verbs work. Rather it concentrates on the meanings and implications of certain choices speakers and writers have to make about the forms of verbs. In chapter 4 we considered how a writer's choice of the passive rather than the active voice can affect the reader's perception of what s/he is being told. Other contrasts signalled by verb-forms may have comparable effects. Being alert to the meanings different verb forms convey is important, therefore, not only for speaking and writing effectively, but also for the development of critical reading skills.

Looking at pupils' writing

Here is an extract from a piece of writing by 16-year-old Abdul, in which he reflects on his ambitions for the future.

> Since year 10 I was thinking what I'm going to do in the
> future. A friend of mine inspired me to become an actor.
> All I was thinking about to become is a banker, because
> my knowledge and skills in maths is quite great.
>   I know that if I become a Hollywood actor I will be rich
> but I don't do acting for the money I do it because
> I find it fun. I wouldn't mind taking rapping as a career
> but I'll love to be an actor more. If I had the advantage to
> be in a hip hop record label then I wouldn't mind at all.

Putting his thoughts on this subject into writing makes some quite complex grammatical demands on Abdul. For one thing, he is juggling references to past, present and future time: though his focus is on the future, he also has to relate that to the present, the moment at which he is writing (e.g. *I know* [now] *that if I become a Hollywood actor* [in future]), and to explain the genesis of his current ambitions he needs to mention things that happened in the past (e.g. *All I was thinking about* [then]). For another thing, the topic calls for Abdul to do quite a bit of speculating, invoking events that are hypothetical rather than actual or inevitable (e.g. *If I become . . . ; I wouldn't mind . . .*).

   While he does by and large enable the reader to follow his thread, there are points in Abdul's text where an editor might want to make some small changes to the surface form:

Table 1

Abdul's version	Edited version
Since year 10 I **was** thinking	Since year 10 I **have been** thinking
All I was thinking about to become **is**	All I was thinking about to become **was**
But **I'll** love to become an actor more	But **I'd** love to become an actor more

These editing changes all relate to the verb-forms Abdul has chosen: they are about the differences between, for instance, *I was thinking* and *I **have been** thinking*, *it **is*** and *it **was***, *I **will** love* and *I **would** love*. These differences relate to the kinds of meanings I mentioned earlier: meanings to do with whether a state of affairs is located in the past, present or future, whether it is completed or ongoing, actual or hypothetical, possible or certain (or conditional on some other state of affairs). To convey these meanings, users of English exploit the verbal systems which are technically known as **modality**, **tense** and **aspect**. Let us look more closely at how these work and why they matter.

Modality

Modality is an umbrella term for the linguistic devices that allow us to convey our assessment of where something falls along the spectrum between real and unreal, possible and impossible, certain and uncertain, believable and incredible. It is what makes the difference between a factual assertion like *unicorns never existed*, and a more guarded view such as *it seems unlikely that unicorns could ever have existed*—or a bolder claim like *the existence of unicorns must always have been a myth*. Modality, then, is a resource speakers and writers use when they are staking claims to knowledge: it allows them to formulate different kinds of claims (e.g. assertions, opinions, hypotheses, speculations) and indicate how committed they are to those claims. The relevance of this for education is obvious: academic discourse is centrally about staking claims to knowledge. To develop a credible academic voice, learners must acquire the skill of making claims in a way that comes across as judicious—neither too weak to carry conviction nor so strong as to ride roughshod over reasonable doubts. This involves, among other things, learning to exploit the resources of linguistic modality.

From the examples I have given it will already be apparent that not all the resources in question are verbs. Many of them are adverbs, like *perhaps*, *probably*, *possibly*, *conceivably*, [*not*] *necessarily*, *inevitably*—or adjectives, used in formulas that qualify a following statement (e.g. *it is 'possible/probable/likely' that* . . . , *It seems 'doubtful' whether* . . .). In English, however, one resource that is very frequently employed is the closed class of modal auxiliary verbs—*can*, *could*, *shall*, *should*, *will*, *would*, *may*, *might* and *must*—which are commonly referred to as just *modals*.

As I noted in chapter 2, modals are peculiar in their form—they do not take any of the normal verb inflections (no *mighted, *shalls or *woulding). (There is a group of so-called *semi-modals*, including *ought*, *need* and *have to*, which are not classed as 'true' modals because they do not have all these formal peculiarities, though they do share functions and meanings with modals.) All the English modals have more than one potential meaning, but as a group, their meanings generally relate to the ideas of ability, willingness, possibility, necessity, certainty, permission, and obligation. To get a sense of what kind and range of meanings we are dealing with, consider what difference the use of a modal, and the choice of modal, makes in the following examples:

Table 2

Without modal	With modal
It is going to rain	It could/may/might/must be going to rain
I don't believe it	I can't/won't/shan't believe it
(You) go to the ball	You can/may/should/must/shall go to the ball

The sentences on the left convey their *force*—how the speaker means them to be taken—very baldly: the first two are presented as unqualified statements of fact and the last as a direct command. The versions on the right, however, present the same basic propositions as—depending which modal is chosen in which context—speculations, suggestions, hypotheses, predictions, convictions and commitments on the part of the speaker.

In the first example, the various modals represent different points on the spectrum from thinking something is possible to believing it is a logical certainty. The modals in the second example express different degrees of (in)ability or (un)willingness to believe something. Those in the last example cover a spectrum from giving someone permission to do something, through imposing on them an obligation to do it (*you should . . . you must*) to the statement *you shall go*, which presents going as a necessary outcome willed by the speaker. 'Will' and 'shall', though English speakers tend to think of them as mainly expressing the meaning of futurity, are often used in this way, to convey the obligation of the hearer and/or the determination of the speaker to make something happen (e.g. *you will stop watching* Big Brother *and finish your homework right now; if you don't like it, you'll just have to lump it; we shall overcome*).

What about Abdul's use of modals in the text we began with? He uses two of them—'will' and 'would'—and he does so for a particular purpose, which is illustrated in the two sentences below:

1. I know that if I become a Hollywood actor I will be rich
2. If I had the advantage to be in a hip hop record label I wouldn't mind at all

These sentences are known as **conditionals**: they have a two-part 'if . . . then . . .' structure, and there is a pattern whereby the verb tense in the 'if' part has a predictable relationship with the modal in the 'then' part. In sentence (1) the 'if' part has a present tense verb ('if I **become**'), and the 'then' part uses 'will':

If X **happens**, then Y **will** happen.

Sentence (2), by contrast, the 'if' clause contains a past tense verb (*if I **had** the advantage . . .*), and the 'then' part uses 'would':

If X **happened**, then Y **would** happen.

This raises an intriguing point about *tense*, which we tend to think of as a system for locating events in past, present or future time. Although their verbs are, respectively, in the present tense and the past tense, *If I **become** a Hollywood actor* and *If I **had** the advantage to be in a hip hop label* are not references to events located in the present and the past, but quite clearly references to potential future events. This might prompt the question: why is one future event represented using a present-tense verb while the other is represented using the past tense? What is the difference between the two?

The answer is that it goes along with the difference between 'will' and 'would': these modals indicate different degrees of probability or likelihood, and the shift from present to past tense mirrors that difference. Tense in English can function as a sort of metaphor in which time-distance stands for other kinds of distance. Through his choice of past or present and 'would' or 'will', Abdul is not shifting the time-reference of the events he discusses, but rather representing one future event—being in a hip hop record label—as a more distant *possibility* than the other—becoming a Hollywood actor. (There is a third type of conditional sentence (known technically as a *counterfactual*) which distances the 'if'-clause even further in time, and which conveys that the events mentioned did *not* take place: *If I **had become** a Hollywood actor I **would have been** rich*.)

These observations may help us to see what the problem is with the third sentence in which Abdul uses modals—*I wouldn't mind taking rapping as a career, but I'll love to be an actor more*. The problem is that he does not maintain a consistent distance from these two possible futures. He presents rapping as a career he 'wouldn't' mind, but acting as one he 'will' love, suggesting that one is a hypothetical possibility and the other a done deal. This has a jarring effect in a sentence that seems to be about assessing the relative attractions of the two options.

Tense

Most people are familiar with the idea that marking *tense* on verbs gives information about the location of events in time. But I have just suggested that the relationship of tense to time is not always straightforward or literal. Here I want to explore that issue further: how does tense work, and what does it do?

In English, speakers and writers have the option of marking verbs for either present tense (e.g. *he **is** the Prince of Denmark*), or past tense (e.g. *he **was** the Prince of Denmark*). We can also leave verbs unmarked for tense (e.g. *to **be** or not to be . . .*). We do not, however, have the option of putting a verb in the future tense. That option does exist in other languages, such as French and its ancestor Latin: these languages have regular sets of inflections that stand to the future as our own *-ed* inflection stands to the past. But English has nothing directly equivalent. Of course, this does not mean that French speakers can discuss the future and English speakers cannot. It just means that the relationship of grammatical tense to time is not a simple matter.

Consider the sentences below. The ones on the left are clearly about past time, and those on the right are clearly about future time; but what—if you concentrate on form rather than meaning—are the tenses of their verbs?

Table 3

Past time	Future time
She left yesterday	She leaves tomorrow
She was leaving yesterday	She is leaving tomorrow
She was going to leave yesterday	She is going to leave tomorrow
	She will leave tomorrow

In the sentences on the left, all the verbs have past tense. In the first example, the main verb 'left' is the past tense form of 'leave'; in the other two, the past-tense marking is not on the main verb but on the auxiliary verb, 'was' (this is the normal place to mark tense if a sentence contains non-modal auxiliaries). In the sentences on the right, however, where the reference is to future time, the first three verbs are in the *present* tense. (I chose sentences with third-person singular subjects as a test of this: sure enough, the main verb 'leaves' and the auxiliary verb 'is' have the -*s* form that marks present tense in the third person singular.) The last sentence does not contain a present tense-marked verb, but uses the modal 'will'. People do sometimes describe 'will' and 'shall' as future tense forms, but as we have already seen, there is more to these modals than the single function of indicating future time; and as the other 'tomorrow' sentences show, they are not the only forms that English speakers use to do that.

The lack of an invariant correspondence between time and tense is not just a peculiarity of statements about future time, where English does not possess a dedicated tense form. English does possess past and present tense forms, but not all past tense verbs refer to past time, and not all present tense verbs refer to present time. For example, people quite often say things like: *I **was wondering** if I could borrow your pen*, when it is clear they mean they want to borrow the pen *now*. It would be possible to formulate the request in the present tense (*I **wonder** if I could borrow your pen*), but using the past tense metaphorically puts more distance between the speaker and the request, making it (even) less direct, more tentative and therefore a notch more polite. It is the same principle we encountered in the discussion of conditional sentences, where *if X **happened*** represents X as a less certain occurrence than *if X **happens***. Present tense is closer, past tense more distant. And this principle can be exploited in the other direction too. Stories about past events may be told in the present tense (called the *historic present* when used in this way) to make them more immediate and vivid: *and yesterday after school, right, we're walking down the road, right, and she comes running up to him and she laughs in his face and she goes* . . . Present tense verbs are also used to express regular occurrences and axiomatic truths, whose reference is not restricted to present time: *she [always] gets up at seven, patience is a virtue, the square of the hypotenuse is equal to the sum of the squares of the other two sides.*

In the national curriculum framework, the subject of verb tenses comes up most frequently in sections dealing with the conventions of non-fictional written genres such as *information*, *explanation*, and *recount*: the first two are said to demand consistent use of present tense verbs while the third requires the past tense to be used consistently. These generic categories are based on analysing the kinds of writing pupils are regularly required to do in subjects such as history, geography and science (e.g. recounting the events that led up to World War II, or explaining the process of cell division), but Abdul's text should remind us they are idealizations—useful points of reference for thinking about writing rather than recipes to be followed mechanically. Many real pieces of writing, particularly in a subject like English, do not fall neatly into a single generic category, and it may not be necessary or desirable for them to be written in a single tense. The question about tense—and for that matter, grammar generally—is not whether a writer's choices conform to a preordained template, but how well they serve the communicative purpose for which they are being employed.

In Abdul's text, where the verbs are fairly evenly divided between past tense (e.g. *A friend of mine inspired me*), present tense (e.g. *I know that* . . .) and modalized (e.g. *I wouldn't mind*), the answer to that question is 'pretty well'. Though in some cases his choice of a specific verb form could be improved on, his shifts of tense (and modality) are generally motivated by the kind of statement he is making—whether it is about past, present or future time and whether it concerns an established fact or a hypothetical possibility. There is only one point in the text where a shift appears entirely unmotivated: *All I **was** thinking about to become **is** a banker.* Unmotivated shifts like this one do call for editing to make the tense consistent, but inconsistency is not a problem if there is a reason for it.

Aspect: perfect and continuous

Aspect, like tense, is broadly to do with time: aspectual distinctions are about things like whether actions are completed or still ongoing, whether they are of current relevance or no longer relevant, whether they occurred at a single point of time or over a longer period, and so on.

When Abdul writes: *since Year 10 I was thinking about what I'm going to do in future*, your intuitive reaction may be to feel there is something not quite right about the combination of 'since Year 10' and 'I was thinking', and that Abdul's meaning would be better expressed by writing *since Year 10 I **have been thinking**. . . .* He is referring to a process (thinking about what to do with his future) that by his own account began at an identifiable point in the past (when he was in Year 10), and which has continued ever *since* that point, by implication right up to the present. This is one of the meanings relating to time for which users of standard British English generally employ the **perfect** (sometimes called *perfective*) aspect, which is formed by using the auxiliary 'have' with a past participle form (e.g. *given, spoken, been*) of the following verb. It distinguishes past actions which remain relevant in the present from those which belong entirely in the past. A prototypical example is the difference between these two sentences:

He has lived in London for more than 15 years *(implication: he still lives there)*

He lived in London for more than 15 years *(implication: he no longer lives there)*

The perfect is often used with other words which relate one point in time to another, like *since, just, yet* and *already*.

Abdul's *Since Year 10 I was thinking* . . . makes use of another aspectual contrast, between **continuous** and non-continuous forms of the verb—in this case, the difference is between 'I was thinking' and 'I thought' (the continuous aspect is formed by using auxiliary 'be' and the *-ing* form of the following verb). As the label implies, the main purpose for which continuous forms are used is to mark actions or states as continuing over a period of time, often with the implication that they are not yet complete. Another term which some writers use for the continuous is the *progressive*, which is apt for another of its common

functions—indicating that one thing was already in progress when
something else happened (*I was reading the paper when my mobile rang*).

Variation in tense and aspect systems

The marking of tense and aspect is something that varies in different
dialects of English. For example, American English speakers are less likely
than British ones to use the perfect in utterances like *I've just finished
work*: they can say, *I just finished work*. They can also say *did you do it
yet?* rather than *have you done it yet?*, and *I already asked him* rather
than *I've already asked him*. Other varieties of English form the perfect
differently from standard English. Once a woman came up to me at a
bus stop in London and said: 'excuse me, how long are you here?' The
question seemed eccentric, as if she thought I was a tourist spending
my holiday in a bus shelter. But the woman was an Irish English speaker,
and what she was actually asking was the classic bus stop question,
equivalent to standard British *how long have you been here?*

An even more striking contrast with the standard English tense-aspect
system is provided by Caribbean **creole languages** such as Jamaican
Creole. Whereas English signals tense and aspect distinctions using a
combination of verb inflections and auxiliary verbs, Jamaican Creole, like
most creoles, uses particles placed before an uninflected verb. The table
below gives an overview of how this works:

Table 4

Particle before verb	Example	English equivalent
—	*Mi ron*	'I run' or 'I ran'
a	*Mi a ron*	'I'm running'
go	*Mi go a ron*	'I'm going to run'
en a (or *ena*)	*Mi ena ron*	'I was running'
en or *did*	*Mi en ron, mi did ron*	'I have run' or 'I had run'

Jamaican Creole does not overtly distinguish between past and present
tense forms—*mi ron* can mean either 'I (habitually) run' or 'I ran'—and
it might seem that this has the potential to lead to ambiguity and
confusion. However, time reference is often inferable from context, and it
is also possible to specify it using means other than grammatical particles

or inflections: for instance adverbial expressions of time like *on Monday*, *these days*, *before the war*. In some varieties of English, expressions of this sort have taken on a quasi-grammatical function marking past time. In Singapore English, for example, we find utterances like these:[1]

> Last time in kampong we are very poor ('in the village we were very
>   poor')
> Last time the trend different. Now change already ('the trend used to
>   be different: now it has changed')

In these examples the phrase 'last time' is functioning like a past tense marker, while 'already' in the second example is an aspect marker, akin to the standard English perfect.

Both English-based creoles and the 'new' Englishes spoken in places like Singapore originated as learned second languages rather than native tongues.[2] Consequently they were influenced on one hand by their users' first languages (African languages in the Caribbean, Chinese or Malay in Singapore) and on the other by strategies which are commonly used by second language-learners to make an unfamiliar language more manageable, such as eliminating inflections and conveying their meanings through separate words or phrases. In fact, the latter is not just a second language learning strategy: standard English has grammatical features which developed in a similar way to Singapore English 'last time'. For instance, the use of 'be going to' as a way of marking some intended future action developed out of the primary sense of the verb 'go', namely 'move from A to B'. In utterances like *I'm going to visit my mother* or *I'm going to buy food*, 'go' originally meant 'go somewhere other than where I am now', but it also logically implied future action. Over time, speakers came to associate this usage more directly with future action, and to use 'be going to' in that sense whether or not the future action involved literally 'going to' anywhere (cf *I'm going to stay at home today*, which announces the intention *not* to move).

Finite and non-finite verbs

In the last two sections we have been exploring the resources offered by tense and aspect systems for representing the time-dimension of events.

One possibility we have not so far considered, however, is leaving verbs temporally *unmarked*. As an illustration of that possibility, here is part of the opening of Charles Dickens's novel *Bleak House*, with the verbs underlined.

> LONDON. Michaelmas Term lately over, and the Lord Chancellor **sitting** in Lincoln's Inn Hall. Implacable November weather. As much mud in the streets as if the waters **had** but newly **retired** from the face of the earth, and it **would** not **be** wonderful to **meet** a Megalosaurus, forty feet long or so, **waddling** like an elephantine lizard up Holborn Hill. Smoke **lowering** down from chimney-pots, **making** a soft black drizzle, with flakes of soot in it as big as full-grown snow-flakes—**gone** into mourning, one **might imagine**, for the death of the sun. Dogs, undistinguishable in mire. Horses, scarcely better; **splashed** to their very blinkers.

Bleak House deals with a civil court-case which has dragged on so interminably as to make time stand still for those involved in it (it is finally concluded by the end of the novel, but the entire sum of money at issue in it has been eaten up by the cost of the legal proceedings). The famous opening description of a damp and foggy London memorably evokes the feeling of stagnation which is one of the novel's themes. While the most immediately obvious techniques used to do this involve vocabulary and imagery (the mud, the soot, the dinosaur waddling through the city) an important part of the effect is created by the grammar—more specifically, by what Dickens does with verbs.

Narrative in a realist novel is most often rendered predominantly in the past tense. If Dickens had adopted that convention, the beginning of the passage above might look something like this:

> In London, Michaelmas term **had** recently **finished** and the Lord Chancellor **was sitting** in Lincoln's Inn. The November weather **was** implacable; there **was** as much mud in the streets as if the waters **had** but newly **retired** from the face of the earth, and it **would** not **have been** wonderful to **meet** a Megalosaurus . . .

Or if he had chosen the historic present as his narrative tense, it might start: *In London, Michaelmas term* ***is*** *over and the Lord Chancellor* ***is*** *sitting in Lincoln's Inn.*

But either of these choices would convey a sense of flow and movement (and in the case of the historic present, immediacy or urgency) that is the opposite of what Dickens wants here. Accordingly he chooses the less conventional strategy of minimizing any kind of tense marking. In some cases he does this by omitting verbs entirely (e.g. *Implacable November weather*). In other cases he uses modals describing hypothetical states (e.g. *it would not have been wonderful, one might imagine*), which are difficult to pin down precisely in time. The most striking thing he does, though, is to exploit the contrast between **finite** verb forms, which are explicitly marked for tense, and **non-finite** verb forms, which are not marked for tense. In contexts where English would normally require the verb to have either past or present tense (that is, **main** rather than **subordinate clauses**, a distinction about which more will be said in chapter 7), he chooses non-finite, tenseless verb forms like

> The Lord Chancellor <u>**sitting**</u> in Lincoln's Inn
> Horses . . . <u>**splashed**</u> to their very blinkers

In traditional grammar, 'sitting' and 'splashed' are called, respectively, the present and past *participle* forms of the verb. This 'present/past' terminology is rather misleading, however, because on their own participle forms have no tense: they acquire tense only when they are combined with auxiliary verbs which are marked for tense, and either participle form can go with either a present tense or a past tense auxiliary. For instance:

> The Lord Chancellor <u>**is**</u> sitting in Lincoln's Inn (*present*)
> The Lord Chancellor <u>**was**</u> sitting in Lincoln's Inn (*past*)

Dickens's alternative—*The Lord Chancellor sitting in Lincoln's Inn*, with no auxiliary and therefore no tense-marking, is less specific about the timing and duration of the state of affairs being described. The accretion of sentences like this produces a kind of 'freeze-frame' effect: the passing of time becomes irrelevant, just as it has become irrelevant to the endless proceedings of the fictional court.

Though it might seem far-fetched to compare them, in some ways 16-year-old Abdul resembles Dickens: he too is making use of tense and modality to enable his reader to imagine what he imagines. The questions with which a reader or a critic finds it natural to approach a passage of Dickens—'what is he trying to do in this piece of text? How is he going about it, and how well does it work?'—are equally good questions for teachers to ask about the writing of their pupils.

Clauses

Looking at pupils' writing

Below is the last paragraph of a story written by Jason, a Year 8 pupil.
The protagonist, Chloe, has stepped through a trapdoor into a parallel
world where she encounters her dead mother:

> She kept walking looking at her mother she said mum
> waiting for a reply her mum answered yes its me Chloe
> Chloe said you suppose to be dead her mum replied yes
> I no but I came back to be with you I had to beg the
> god for another chance he only let me be with u if u stay
> in hear with me so are u going to stay with me Chloe
> answered no mum I have got a life I can't stay hear
> with u because you are not real and said bye mum and
> ran out the house crying.

Jason is evidently uncertain about the nature of the sentence as a unit
of written language. The unit of writing he operates with confidently
is the paragraph: his story consists of three paragraphs, which might
be characterized as (1) scene-setting, (2) complicating action, and
(3) denouement. Within these paragraphs, however, he does not
explicitly subdivide the text into sentences by using capitalization
and punctuation marks.

This is quite a common feature of texts produced by developing
writers: in chapter 4 we looked at another text—the pupil's story about
breaking his arm—which also marked off paragraphs with initial capitals/
final full stops, but did not put in any internal sentence boundaries. If we
look at that text again, though, we will notice that in other ways it is
very different from Jason's story.

> *My first time I broke my arm because I was riding a bike and my brother got in the way of the bike so my arm went on the wheel and my dad took me to my nan's to get a car to the hospital and my brothers went to see my mum in the pub and I went to the hospital with my dad and I sleep in the hospital for 6 weeks and I went home and the next day I went to school and I did not write or do no work I play on the computer in the classroom.*

I pointed out before that putting sentence boundaries into this text would involve some fairly arbitrary decisions about how to divide it up. For instance, all three of the following would be possible arrangements of the last part:

1. And the next day I went to school, and I did not write or do no work. I play on the computer in the classroom.
2. And the next day I went to school. And I did not write or do no work. I play on the computer in the classroom.
3. And the next day I went to school. I did not write or do no work, I play on the computer in the classroom.

The grammar permits all of these, but gives us no special reason to prefer any of them.

Jason's story is different. It may not be punctuated explicitly, but it is put together grammatically in a way that tells us far more about where the important boundaries are. For instance: *She kept walking, looking at her mother. She said 'Mum', waiting for a reply.* Or: *Yes, I know, but I came back to be with you. I had to beg the god for another chance. He only let me be here with you if you stay in here with me. So are you going to stay with me?*

The difference between the two texts is to do with the way certain units of grammatical structure, **clauses**, are related to one another. The broken arm narrative is an example of **parataxis**, a structure where clauses are put together using either **coordination** (in this case, 'and . . . and . . . and . . .') or simple juxtaposition without an explicit connective word (as in *I did not write or do no work/ I play on the computer in the* *classroom*). Jason's story makes more use of **hypotaxis**, a hierarchical form of organization where instead of all the clauses being equal, some are *subordinate* to others. An example is *She kept walking, <u>looking at her mother</u>*. The first bit is the main clause and the underlined part is a subordinate clause (I will come back to what these terms mean and how we know which is which). Other examples include *I came back <u>to be with you</u>*, and *I can't stay here with you <u>because you are not real</u>*.

The broken arm story does contain a few subordinate clauses: *My first time I broke my arm <u>because I was riding a bike</u>*, and *my dad took me to my nan's <u>to get a car to the hospital</u>*. These are used to convey meanings of cause and effect or action and reason. But mostly what the writer conveys by linking clauses with 'and' is the idea of one thing happening after another, with each event in the sequence receiving equal emphasis. That is why, for long stretches of the text, we cannot easily decide where the sentence boundaries should be.

You might ask: but is sentence structure the real problem here? One of the things that make this narrative less than compelling is the writer's lack of selectivity about what is recounted: the principle seems to be that if he remembers it, it goes in, however peripheral it is to the main action (e.g. *my brothers went to see my mum in the pub*). A teacher might well feel that the most important thing to work on is the content, not the grammar. But there is a connection. Joining clauses together in different ways is not just a stylistic trick for making prose less monotonous: it allows writers (and therefore readers) to make distinctions between foreground and background, main storyline and incidental detail. For instance, Jason's *she kept walking, looking at her mother* puts Chloe's walking in the foreground; *still walking, she looked at her mother*, would make the walking more incidental and foreground the act of looking. In the 'and . . . and . . . and . . .' structure, however (*she kept walking and she looked at her mother and she said . . .*), nothing matters more than anything else: everything is presented for the reader's attention in exactly the same way.

This form of organization can be effective for some purposes, but in the broken arm narrative no particular effect has been aimed for: the writer has simply transcribed his recollections without reworking them in any way. He is evidently struggling with the challenge of writing for someone else: to become more accomplished as a writer, he must develop more of a sense of audience, and an imaginary relationship to his audience which enables him to shape his thoughts in response to the reader's interests, expectations and state of knowledge. Knowing how to write for someone who is not inside your own head is something many less accomplished writers find particularly difficult, and the problem is not primarily to do with grammar. Nevertheless, grammar will be part of the solution to it. To make his writing clearer and more interesting for a reader, this writer will need, among other things, to learn to break up a narrative into more manageable chunks, and to convey to the reader what is more or less central by diverging from the 'and . . . and . . . and . . .' structure. Jason still has things to learn about spelling and punctuation, but this is one thing he seems to have cracked.

Main and subordinate clauses

A *clause* is a unit of grammatical structure which is bigger than a phrase but potentially smaller than a whole sentence. Some whole sentences consist of just one clause, but many consist of more than one. The easiest way to tell how many clauses there are in a given sentence or stretch of discourse is to count the verbs. Wherever there is a verb, there is a clause. In the following examples I have highlighted the verbs and marked the clause boundaries using slashes:

1. And I **sleep** in the hospital for 6 weeks
2. And I **went** to school/ and **I did not write**/ or **do** no work/
   I **play** on the computer in the classroom
3. My dad **took** me to my nan's/ to **get** a car to the hospital
4. As she **was getting** closer/ she **heard** some strange noises
   of music
5. She **saw** her mum/ that **has been** dead for 6 months
6. I **came** back/ to **be** with you
7. I **can't stay** here with you/ because you **are** not real
8. Chloe **ran** out of the house/ **crying**

Notice that I have highlighted auxiliary verbs along with the main verb they precede (e.g. 'did' in *I did not write*, 'was' in *as she was getting closer*, 'has' in *that has been dead for 6 months*, and 'can't' in *I can't stay here with you*). Since these are not main verbs, they are not counted separately.

Verb-counting tells us how many clauses there are, but how do we tell the difference between main clauses and subordinate clauses? The traditional guidance on this point says that a main clause is one that could stand on its own (i.e. if you removed everything else it would still be a complete sentence), whereas a subordinate clause is *dependent* on a main clause and would therefore be incomplete on its own. For example, in sentences (5) and (6) above, 'She saw her mum' and 'I came back' could stand as sentences in their own right, but 'That has been dead for 6 months' and 'To be with you' could not. In sentence (2) on the other hand, every clause could stand as a sentence in its own right: they are all main clauses (the term 'main clause' might seem to imply that there should only be one per sentence, but in fact there can be more: the rule is 'at least one'). This is why we feel that every event in the broken arm story is being given equal weight.

The 'can it stand alone' test for main/subordinate clauses works up to a point, but it does throw up some anomalies. Consider, for instance, the familiar advertising slogan for L'Oreal cosmetics: *Because you're worth it*. As we will see in a moment, this is a subordinate clause, but how many people would judge it intuitively as incomplete, or cast around for the 'missing' main clause? Conversely, in a sentence like *I thought it was stupid*, the main clause ('I thought') seems rather less capable of standing on its own than the subordinate clause ('it was stupid'). The most reliable diagnostics work on the basis of form rather than meaning, and at this point I will turn to the formal characteristics of subordinate clauses.

One indicator of whether a clause is main or subordinate is what kind of **conjunction** (or **connective**) introduces it. If main clauses do not 'stand alone' as separate sentences, they will often be linked by *coordinating conjunctions*, the most common being *and*, *or* and *but*. Subordinate clauses, on the other hand, will not be introduced by coordinating conjunctions like *and*, but they may be introduced by **subordinating conjunctions** such as *because, since, (al)though, if, as, while, when, after*:

> I can't stay here with you **because** you are not real
> **Since** you are not real, I can't stay here with you
> **Although** she was dead, Chloe's mother came back
> I can't stay **if** you aren't real
> **As** she was getting closer she heard some strange noises of music.
> **While** she was waiting she looked at her mother.
> **After** she ran out of the house, Chloe burst into tears.

There is no rule about whether main or subordinate clauses come first, and in all the above examples, the order I have put them in could be reversed. The last example, for instance, could equally well have been *Chloe burst into tears after she ran out of the house*. The sequence of clauses does not have to mirror the sequence of events, because the 'after' itself makes the chronology clear. In the coordinated, 'and . . . and . . . and . . .' -type narrative, by contrast, not recounting events in order of their occurrence will lead to confusion. *He tripped and fell in the river and drowned* is a perfectly sensible sentence, but *he drowned and fell in the river and tripped* is bizarre. By using the right subordinating conjunctions, however, you can put the events in any order, e.g. *he drowned after he fell in the river because he tripped*. 'After', 'while' and 'when' are conjunctions that express relations of time; other conjunctions may express relations of cause and effect (e.g. 'because', 'if'). The coordinating conjunctions 'or' and 'but' also express logical relationships between the entities they link: 'or' for instance signals that the things on either side of it are alternatives. But the commonest coordinator, 'and', is also the one that is least specific about the nature of the connection it makes.

   Another type of subordinate clause structure is introduced by 'that':

> Chloe's mother said/that she had begged God for another chance
> Chloe told her mother/that she could not stay
> Chloe thought/that she was dreaming
> She decided/that she couldn't give up everything
> She was so glad/that Chloe could come
> It was a pity/that she ran away

In all these examples you would have the option of leaving out the 'that' (e.g. *She thought she was dreaming*), and in some cases it would be more natural to do so. But if you encounter this type of structure without a 'that', it will still be possible to insert one at the beginning of the subordinate clause. This tells you that there is a slot in the structure for 'that', it is just that filling it is optional. 'That'-insertion will also serve as a test allowing you to distinguish the main clause from the subordinate clause (the subordinate clause is the one you can put 'that' before).

The type of sentence we have just looked at might remind you of something that was discussed in chapter 5: the *relative clause*, as in *the house that Jack built*, which can also be introduced with 'that' (or a WH- word like 'which', 'why', 'when', 'where'—or nothing, as in *the house Jack built*). A relative clause is indeed a type of subordinate clause: its distinctive feature, however, which differentiates it from the examples above, is that a relative clause is totally contained inside a noun phrase, and follows (postmodifies) a noun rather than a clause like *she felt/thought/said* or *she was glad/amused/amazed*. This chapter has already supplied the reason why it has to be analysed as a clause despite being embedded in a phrase: it's because there is a verb in it. If you count the main verbs in the sentence *this is the house that Jack built*, there are two, so there must also be two clauses. (*This is the house/ that Jack built*.)

We saw in chapter 5 that relative clauses are recursive structures which can be recycled over and over to build more and more levels of hierarchy (or embed more and more Russian dolls inside each other)—the result being longer and longer sequences (e.g. *this is the cow with the crumpled horn that tossed the dog that worried the cat that killed the rat that ate the malt . . .*). Other kinds of subordinate clause structures have the same potential to keep being recycled. For instance, soldiers in World War I used to sing, to the tune of *Auld Lang Syne*: 'we're here because we're here because we're here because we're here'; a forthcoming film starring Jim Carrey is titled *I know that you know that I know*; I overheard a mobile phone conversation this week in which the caller said: 'just tell him to remind me to ask her to call him'.

This last example illustrates another type of subordinate clause where the clue is in the form of the verb: specifically, the fact that it is *non-finite*, does not have a tense. Here are some examples, with the subordinate clauses underlined:

I came back/<u>to be with you</u>
God has let me/<u>come back</u>
Chloe ran out of the house/<u>crying</u>
The vase was lying/<u>broken</u>

In each of these examples, the main clause verb has some kind of tense marking, either on the main verb (e.g. *I came* [past]) or the auxiliary verb (e.g. *has let* [present perfect] and *was lying* [past continuous]). But the verbs in the subordinate clauses are not present or past tense forms. The first two are uninflected or **infinitive** forms (*to be, come*—the first has the explicit infinitive marker 'to', the second is a so-called 'bare' infinitive, with no 'to'). The second two, as I explained in chapter 6, are *participle* forms. These inflected forms do occur in contexts where the verb has a tense, e.g. *was lying* and *has let*, but in these cases it is the auxiliary verb that tells us if the sentence is in the present or past tense: if they occur without preceding auxiliary verbs, participle forms themselves have no tense.

The distinction between finite and non-finite is important for the definition of main clauses and therefore sentences. A main clause has to have a finite verb—one which is marked, whether on the main verb or an auxiliary verb, as being either present or past tense. A subordinate clause may have either a finite or a non-finite verb. It follows that if a clause has a non-finite verb it can only be a subordinate clause. It also follows that a complete sentence, since it has to contain at least one main clause, must also contain at least one finite, tensed verb. That is why my secondary school grammar teacher, back in the days when schools taught traditional 'clause analysis', informed us that *the dog ran* is a complete sentence and *the dog running* is not. We found this puzzling, since we had also been taught that a complete sentence needs a subject and a verb. *The dog running* seems to conform to that rule just as well as *the dog ran*. What the teacher failed to explain was that any old verb won't do: it has to be marked for tense. *The dog running* has no tense: that means it is not a main clause but a subordinate clause, which can only ever be *part* of a complete sentence (e.g. *I saw the dog running*). A complete sentence needs at least one main clause, and a main clause requires not just a verb but a finite verb.

The table below gives a summary of the information presented in this section about subordinate clauses.

Table 1

Subordinate clause characteristics	Examples	Comments
Introduced by subordinating conjunction, e.g. *because, since, as, while, after, when, if*	*If I knew*, I would tell you. Hillary climbed Everest *because it was there*	
Introduced by *that* (or zero)	I'm glad *(that) you asked* I presume *(that) you are Dr Livingstone*	If there's no 'that' you will be able to add one
Introduced by relative pronoun, e.g. *that* (or zero), *which, who, when, why*	The dog *that ate my homework* The woman *my cousin married*	Postmodifies a noun and is contained within a NP
Infinitive, with or without 'to'	She wanted *to go home* I made her *go home*	Non-finite
Participle, *-ing* or *-en*	They stood around *staring* They stood around, *shocked*	Non finite

For practice, self-assessment and discussion

The following text, written by a classmate of Jason's, is the opening of another scary story about a trapdoor. See if you can divide it up into clauses (by identifying the verbs and then working out which chunks of text belong with each); then find all the examples of subordinate clauses (by looking for formal clues such as subordinating conjunctions, relative pronouns and non-finite verb forms). My solution is in the notes.[1]

> Bobby went to get his football from the garden because he forgot to bring it inside earlier that day when he was playing football with his brother. So he opened the door in the kitchen and came out it was pouring with rain he looked for it and after a few moments he saw it. He ran to get it while he was running he slipped and fell on the muddy grass or did he.

> *He looked [at] the place he fell there was no stones there*
> *only grass it was something else he wiped his hand through*
> *the grass and the grass went to the side and he saw a*
> *handle and a boxed shaped door or maybe a trapdoor.*

In the next part of the story Bobby's mother tells him to come in out of the rain and he is prevented from opening the trapdoor. Here is the section that follows. The question I invite you to consider is: how effectively does the writer exploit the various possibilities he has available for making connections between clauses—juxtaposition, coordination, subordination? What is done well, and what needs to be worked on?

> *When Bobby went to bed that night he had all thoughts*
> *waving around his head and all sorts of stuff and questions*
> *he wanted to know.*
> *What was that box shaped door?*
> *Was it a trap door?*
> *What was in there?*
> *Why was it there?*
> *The next morning when [he] woke he was exhausted he*
> *went down to the kitchen to eat his breakfast he realised*
> *it wasn't raining anymore the sun was shining brightly on*
> *the kitchen when he remembered the trapdoor he couldn't*
> *find it it was gone he thought of the possibility that he was*
> *in a dream.*

The list of questions is an example of the effective use of parataxis— a style, as noted earlier, which uses juxtaposition and coordination rather than hierarchical structures with subordinate clauses. In this case it takes the form of repeated simple (one-clause) sentences which just follow one after the other, without any explicit linking. Here, though, the paratactic structure serves a purpose. Rather than just mirroring the writer's own thought processes, this series of questions does something for the reader by mirroring the character's thoughts. It dramatizes the idea the writer has already introduced, of Bobby lying in bed with all kinds of questions 'waving around his head'. Using direct questions (and leaving them unanswered) also contributes to the creation of suspense. An indirect question like *he asked himself what that box shaped door was and whether it was a trapdoor* would be more complex grammatically, but it would also distance the reader from Bobby's thoughts and lessen the dramatic tension, making the passage overall less effective. Hypotaxis is not always automatically preferable to parataxis—another illustration of the more general point that good writing is not about ticking a pre-ordained set of grammatical boxes (e.g. adjectives, consistent verb tenses, subordinate clauses), it is about choosing the right grammatical tools for the job a writer has set out to do.

After the list of questions, this writer's choices about how to organize his text grammatically become rather less effective, despite the fact that he continues to use a fairly wide range of clause structures. Like Jason, he does not break paragraphs into sentences using punctuation, and in the last paragraph above it isn't always clear where he means the sentence boundaries—as opposed to the clause boundaries—to be. Is it *the sun was shining brightly on the kitchen when he remembered the trapdoor. He couldn't find it—it was gone* or is it *the sun was shining brightly on the kitchen. When he remembered the trapdoor, he couldn't find it—it was gone*? It is clear from the grammar how many clauses there are, but not how they fit together. The writer needs to become more accomplished in doing with punctuation what he would do in speech with prosody (getting him to read the text aloud might help to clarify what goes with what).

He could also improve the text by drawing on a wider range of options for linking clauses at the beginning of the paragraph, to avoid the rather plodding *He went down to the kitchen to eat breakfast. He realised it wasn't raining anymore. The sun was shining brightly. . . .* He has already used a 'when' clause in the first sentence, but an 'as' before 'he went down to the kitchen' would allow him to join all these clauses in one sentence (*as he went down to the kitchen to eat his breakfast he realised it wasn't raining anymore*). This kind of structure would also relegate the mundane and predictable activity of going downstairs for breakfast to the status of background, while foregrounding the point that advances the main narrative, namely that the rain has stopped, giving Bobby the opportunity to go back to the trapdoor and discover that it has inexplicably vanished.

8 | Dialects

Below is an extract from DH Lawrence's novel *Lady Chatterley's Lover* ('he' is the gamekeeper Mellors; 'she' is Lady Chatterley):

> 'Tha mun come one naight ter th'cottage, afore tha goos; sholl ter?' he asked.
>
> . . . 'Sholl ter?' she echoed, teasing.
>
> He smiled.
>
> 'Ay, sholl ter?' he repeated.
>
> 'Ay', she said, imitating the dialect sound.
>
> 'Appen a' Sunday', she said.
>
> 'Appen a' Sunday! Ay!' He laughed at her quickly.
>
> 'Nay, tha canna', he protested.
>
> 'Why canna I?' she said.
>
> He laughed. Her attempts at the dialect were so ludicrous, somehow.

This illustrates both the popular stereotype and the more technical meaning of the term **dialect**. Stereotypically, 'dialect' is the traditional folk-speech of uneducated rural people. More technically, '*a* dialect' is a **variety** of a language which is distinguished from other varieties, not just by the **accent** it is pronounced with, but also by its vocabulary and its grammar. For instance, Mellors's dialect includes the traditional **lexical** (word) variants '(h)appen' ('perhaps') and 'mun' ('must'); it uses the -*s* inflection to mark the present tense in the second person singular form of the verb (*tha goos*); and it preserves the old grammatical distinction between singular 'thou' (here spelt 'tha') and plural 'you'. That distinction also used to function in English like the difference between familiar '*tu*' and polite '*vous*' in French. Mellors's use of singular/familiar 'thou' to

Lady Chatterley is a clue to the intimate—and socially transgressive— nature of their relationship.

The fact that Mellors speaks the dialect whereas Lady Chatterley does not is also a reflection of the class difference between them. The gamekeeper uses a local form of **non-standard English** (NSE); the lady of the manor speaks the non-localized, *social* dialect known as **standard English** (SE). In this passage, unusually, it is the SE speaker's inability to speak NSE which is portrayed as a problem. More commonly, though, it is lower status speakers like Mellors who are disparaged as speaking 'incorrect' or 'bad' English.

This judgement reflects not only class prejudice, but also the influence of literacy. Because literate people treat the written form as their model for all language, the grammar of written English becomes their model for judging grammatical correctness. That, in turn, means treating the standard dialect as the norm, because SE is the only dialect which is used consistently in writing. NSE is often found in literary texts, but we do not encounter scientific journal articles in Cumbrian, history textbooks in Bristolian, financial reports in East Anglian or computer manuals in Cockney. In order to become literate, therefore, children whose home variety of English is a local non-standard dialect must also develop competence in SE.

The national curriculum places great emphasis on cultivating standard language competence. It requires pupils to use SE 'fluently and accurately', in informal speech as well as writing, and to have their attention drawn explicitly to the grammatical differences between SE and NSE so they are clear about which forms they should use and which they should avoid. In chapter 1 I suggested that this preoccupation with standard English is a legacy of the political debates of the 1980s. Though some aspects of it are uncontroversial (no one, for instance, disputes the pre-eminence of SE as a written medium), others are more contentious. To help teachers make their own assessment of this part of the national curriculum, I will focus in this chapter on what we know about the reality of dialect variation in English. A good place to start is with some history.

English dialects and the English language

What we now call 'non-standard' dialects—geographically distinct varieties of English—go back much further in time than SE. For centuries after the English language was first brought to Britain in the early Middle Ages, dialects were all that existed: there was no 'standard English' serving the communicative needs of the whole nation. For much of this period, indeed, there was no unified English nation.

In England as elsewhere, it was the emergence of a nation which prompted the creation of a linguistic standard. Once you establish a political unit that is large enough to be non-uniform linguistically, the need arises for a medium of communication that can be used throughout the territory, making the same documents comprehensible whether their readers are in Canterbury or Corbridge. This is an impetus to the development of a nationwide standard for writing. In England that development was underway by the 14th century.

The first stage of standardization is to select a dialect to become the standard. Though the chosen variety will lose its local associations in the process of being standardized, it starts off as just another local dialect: in the case of English, the southeastern midland dialect used by the London courtly and merchant classes. That dialect was not selected because of any special linguistic qualities, but rather because its users included the economic and political elite. (Had the process happened a few centuries earlier, the obvious choice for exactly the same reason would have been the dialect spoken around Winchester, capital of the kingdom of Wessex.) Once a dialect has been selected, it then needs to be equipped for its role through *elaboration* (see chapter 3), which expands its vocabulary and stylistic resources so that it can fulfil all the necessary communicative functions, and *codification* (see chapter 1), which involves writing down the rules of the new standard to enable them to be followed consistently. In the case of English, these processes occurred largely in the early modern period (c.1500–1750); because languages change, however, the maintenance of a standard is an ongoing task, and the same processes continue on a smaller scale today.

The consequences of standardization were far-reaching, not only for the 'chosen' dialect, but also for those which were *not* chosen. The elaboration of one dialect to fulfil all functions means that other dialects are stripped of any high-status functions they had before. If they had written forms, as several English dialects did during the Middle Ages, they lose them. They are reduced to *patois*, the unwritten everyday language of the uneducated. Consequently they begin to be thought of as common, unrefined, inferior—and in time, when the standard is established in people's minds as the norm for the whole language, as 'corrupt' and 'deviant' forms which have no grammar of their own, but are rather collections of errors stemming from carelessness, ignorance and lack of logic.

Today's local dialects are of course different from the ones that existed in the Middle Ages, the 18ᵗʰ century, or even the 1920s, when Lawrence wrote *Lady Chatterley's Lover*. In the pre-industrial era, most people lived and worked in the countryside, had minimal contact with anyone beyond their own locality, and often could not read or write. These conditions produced sharply delineated local rural dialects, with speakers who used their own dialect consistently. But social changes during the past 200 years—for instance urbanization, industrialization, mobility and mass education—have led to the gradual loss of *traditional* rural dialects and monodialectal speakers. Today the most widely spoken NSE dialects are urban rather than rural, and are used more variably than the traditional dialects of the past.

The English varieties spoken in and around Britain's cities are the results of population-mixing during industrialization, when large numbers of people migrated to work in urban mills and factories. Many came from the surrounding countryside, giving urban dialects continuity with the traditional dialect of their region; but some came from outside the area, making the cities dialectal 'melting pots'. When speakers of different dialects interact extensively, the sharpest differences between them tend to be reduced (the technical term for this is **levelling**), and if there are enough speakers of any particular dialect, it will contribute something to the new mix (for instance, Liverpool English has clearly been influenced by the presence of large numbers of Irish migrants). Since the industrial revolution, dialect levelling has continued (the spread of so-called 'Estuary English' across southeast England is one recent product of it). Other changes that have affected language and language-use include the development of better communications, the arrival of new migrant groups from all over the world, and the extension of educational opportunities—and thus literacy in standard English—from a small elite to the mass of the population. Because of these changes, we no longer have dialects with sharply drawn boundaries and monodialectal speakers; instead we have dialects which influence one another and speakers who can draw on a repertoire of forms.

Sociolinguistic patterns: the structure of modern dialect variation

Rather than being completely non-standard or standard, most modern English-speakers' linguistic behaviour shows *variation*—they make some use of both SE and NSE forms, but in differing proportions depending on various social factors. One of the most important of these is a speaker's social class. The table below is taken from a study of speakers in Norwich[1], where one feature of the local dialect is that third person singular present tense verbs do not have the *-s* inflectional ending: it's *he go*, not *he goes*. The table shows the percentage of non-standard forms used by speakers of different classes.

Table 1

Speaker's social class	% Non-standard verb forms
Upper middle class	0
Lower middle class	2
Upper working class	70
Middle working class	87
Lower working class	97

The pattern displayed in this table is technically known as *sharp stratification*. **Stratification** means a regular pattern whereby the proportion of standard forms rises along with the social status of the speaker. In this case, middle-class speakers use virtually no non-standard verb forms (in the upper middle class, none at all), but among working-class speakers the non-standard forms are dominant. In the lowest-status group their incidence is close to 100%. The stratification is termed 'sharp' because of the huge jump in standard usage (from 30% to 98%) between the upper working class and lower middle class. Some forms show 'fine stratification', a more gradual increase in standard usage as you move up the social scale. But stratification itself is a pervasive sociolinguistic pattern.

Another pervasive pattern is known as **styleshifting**. In all groups whose behaviour shows variation, the frequency of standard forms rises as the situation becomes more formal. Non-standard forms are most frequent when people are chatting casually to friends and family, or when they get carried away with telling a story or joke. In other situations they will tend to use a higher proportion of standard forms.

There is also a pattern relating to age or life-stage. In most communities it will usually be working adults, rather than children, retired or unemployed people, who use the highest proportions of standard forms. This is because work typically takes people out of their immediate locality and brings them into regular contact with people from outside their own group. Even if a job does not intrinsically require the use of SE (and many jobs do exert pressure in that direction), talking in institutional settings and to people you are not close to favours more use of standard forms. Non-standard forms, conversely, are used most consistently within tight-knit, locally based networks of kin and close friends. People who do not work spend more of their time in these networks.

Childhood and adolescence are times when peer-interaction is both very intense and usually very locally based, since young people do not have adults' freedom of movement. It is often assumed that adolescents' use of language is most influenced by the media (and that consequently British adolescents are heavily influenced by the US varieties which they encounter through music, films and TV). But a recent study of secondary school pupils in Tower Hamlets, East London, confirmed that it is local factors which have the greatest impact on language.[2] Many features of the Tower Hamlets pupils' speech reflected the local influence of Bangladeshi culture and the Bengali language. Similarly, Gautam Malkani's novel *Londonstani* represents its protagonists, young Asian men in the west London suburb of Hounslow, using a variety of English that mixes Punjabi and Jamaican influences:

> Ansa me you dutty gora, Hardjit goes, before kneeling down an
>   punchin him in the mouth . . .
> — Dat's right, the three a us go in boy-band mode again,—ansa da
>   man or we bruck yo f***in face.
> — Yeh blud, safe, goes Ravi.

The importance of local influences also reflects the close connection between language and identity—a matter of particularly intense concern for many adolescents. Like clothing and musical tastes, the way you speak is a resource for communicating to others who you are, what place and group you belong to, who you want to be like and who you want to be different from. In places like Tower Hamlets and Hounslow, young people of all ethnicities draw from the various languages and dialects that are used within the local community (e.g. Bengali or Punjabi, Asian English, Cockney, London Jamaican) to signal the affiliations and distinctions that are meaningful in their social world.[3] For the Asians in *Londonstani*, for instance, using Punjabi says something about their ethnic roots, but mixing it with Jamaican signifies their identification as 'rude boys' and their rejection of the more conformist Asian identity which they disparagingly label 'coconut' ('brown on the outside, white on the inside').

'Spoken standard English'?

When the Tower Hamlets study was reported in the media, it was also reported that one London school had banned the variety of English the research was about, as part of a drive to improve standards. The head teacher was quoted as saying: 'Where children drop into anything that isn't standard they are picked up on it'. He added that he was not devaluing the dialect, but 'trying to teach the kids there's a time and a place for it'.[4] This intervention is arguably in the spirit of the national curriculum, which says that pupils should be taught to use spoken SE in both informal and formal contexts. Yet in the light of what has just been said about sociolinguistic patterns, we might have questions about that very broad requirement.

Research suggests that secondary school-age pupils already understand that there is a time and a place for different ways of speaking: the evidence is that they engage in styleshifting. But if pupils can shift to a more standard way of speaking in certain situations—for instance, addressing teachers and participating in formal classroom discussions—then there is nothing to be gained from prohibiting NSE in informal speech situations such as casual conversation among peers. What that strategy overlooks is that there are contexts where NSE is appropriate and SE is not. If we want pupils to appreciate the importance of SE for some purposes, we need to acknowledge that it does not necessarily serve all their purposes equally well: it is no use, for instance, to a speaker whose concern at that moment is to demonstrate his credentials as a rude boy and not a coconut. Of course it is important that pupils who have little contact with SE outside school should get plenty of practice using it in school; but prohibiting NSE in all contexts is not the best way to ensure this. Rather, the answer is to create contexts and design activities in which it is genuinely more appropriate and more effective to use SE.

Even then, it is unrealistic to expect SE forms to be used with 100% consistency in speech. Some sociolinguists have argued that the whole concept of 'spoken standard English' is problematic, because it is so unclear what counts as 'standard' in speech as opposed to writing. The defining feature of a standard dialect is that it has undergone the process of standardization, a key part of which involves codifying rules in sources like dictionaries, grammars and usage guides. But the object of codifiers' attention is always the written rather than the spoken form of the language. Since speech differs in many ways from writing (I will explore these differences further in chapter 9), many of the rules made for the written language either do not apply to speech or are ignored in practice by the majority of speakers. Studies of spoken *corpora* (very large samples of naturally occurring speech) have shown that even highly educated middle-class speakers frequently break what are supposed to be basic rules of SE grammar. To give just one example, it is far more common to say *where's my keys?* and *there's two men at the door* than to follow the **subject-verb agreement** rule laid down in prescriptive grammar texts, according to which plural nouns like 'keys' and 'men' require the plural verb form 'are'.

What should we conclude from this? If we conclude that *where's my keys* is 'standard' in speech—despite the fact that it would not be accepted as such in writing—we are essentially defining 'spoken standard English' as 'whatever middle-class speakers say', and non-standard speech by implication as anything middle-class speakers do not say. (When working-class speakers break the same subject-verb agreement rule by saying *we was looking for the keys*, no one suggests that they are speaking anything but NSE.) But if we conclude that *where's my keys* is 'non-standard', we are attaching a stigma to what in fact is most English-speakers' normal usage. A more sensible conclusion might be that speech is by nature far more variable than writing, and that consequently 'spoken standard English' is not a well-defined linguistic entity: it can only really mean a way of speaking that is influenced by the norms of the written standard. The extent of that influence will vary: some tasks (e.g. making a planned oral presentation to a large group) call for a kind of speech which strongly resembles writing, in grammatical complexity and formality of tone as well as standardness; others (e.g. story- or joke-telling) call for something entirely different. Once again, 'there's a time and a place'.

In the course of this discussion of spoken language, the question may have occurred to you: what about accent? Is it not the case that in speech, SE and NSE will be distinguished most obviously by the way they are pronounced? The answer is not straightforward. People who speak a local dialect (i.e. use non-standard grammar and vocabulary) will invariably do so with the associated local accent (pronunciation); but equally, people who do not speak a local dialect may have a local accent.

There is an accent of British English, known as **received pronunciation** or **RP**, which like the standard dialect is non-localized, a badge of class rather than regional provenance (it is used by the royal family, and by many people who were educated at public schools.) But RP-speakers are a very small minority (estimates range from 2% to 5% of the population). Most middle-class English-speakers have some kind of mild-to-moderate local accent, perhaps influenced by RP but not directly exemplifying it. RP thus cannot be thought of as simply the phonological component of SE. Nor, given its very strong class connotations, can it make the same claims that are made for SE as an 'inclusive' variety, accepted and used for at least some purposes by everyone.

When the national curriculum says that pupils should be taught to use SE in speech, it does not mean they should be taught RP. This is evident from the wording of the relevant requirements, which stipulate 'the vocabulary, structures and grammar' of SE, with no mention at all of pronunciation. It was once quite common for schools to teach RP under the heading of 'elocution' or 'speech training', but in today's less snobbish climate few educators would see this as either necessary or desirable.

But whatever position we take on the issue of 'spoken standard English'—whether it exists, what it is, and in what contexts (if any) it might be important for schoolchildren to use it—it is difficult to dispute the educational importance of standard English as the dialect of writing. In writing, pupils do need to be able to use SE grammar consistently, and teachers therefore need to know how the grammatical systems of other dialects may differ from that of SE. At this point, then, let us turn to the actual substance of the differences. Here it needs to be borne in mind that non-standard dialects are different from one another as well as from the standard. Space does not permit me to describe all the features of every local dialect: I can only concentrate on the kinds of things that tend to vary, with some examples, and invite readers to compare the dialects they are dealing with to my illustrations.

Standard and non-standard grammar

Before I turn to specifics, though, I need to explain what I meant when I referred above to dialects having differing grammatical *systems*. As I noted earlier, non-standard forms are often seen as just errors, deviating in random and illogical ways from the norm represented by the standard. It is important to understand why this perception is misguided, so let us focus on a concrete case.

Consider Mellors's *afore tha goos*. Characterizing this as an 'error' implies that it is a failed attempt to produce SE *before you go*. Apart from being inherently implausible (how could you aim for one and accidentally produce the other?) this does not explain why *afore tha goos* has the structure it has, or why everyone else in Mellors's community makes exactly the same 'mistake'. These speakers are not trying and failing to conform to the rules of SE, but following the rules of another grammatical system—one in which, for instance, the second person pronoun has to be marked for number (singular or plural), and all present tense verbs have to be inflected with -*s*. The non-standard dialect has rules for the same things as the standard dialect, but either the rules are slightly different or the grammatical forms on which they operate are.

Connie's *why canna I?*, by contrast, really *is* a failed attempt to speak a dialect whose rules she does not know. She reasons that NSE 'canna' is like SE 'can't'—that you form questions by moving it in front of the subject, as in *why can't I?* But in fact, 'canna' is equivalent to SE 'cannot' rather than the contracted form 'can't'. Just as SE speakers would not say *why cannot I?*, so NSE speakers would not say *why canna I?* Mellors laughs because in his dialect this is a mistake, an ungrammatical sequence. Just because non-standard dialects do not have *codified* rules, we should not imagine that they do not have rules at all.

Most dialect differences in present-day English are along the lines of the examples just discussed: they involve relatively superficial variations in either the morphological forms of a word (e.g. its inflectional endings) or the rules for syntactic processes affecting those forms (e.g. negation). There are varieties of English used in Britain (Scots, for example, and those which have developed out of Caribbean creoles) which for historical reasons do differ grammatically from other dialects in deeper ways (an example is the creole tense and aspect system mentioned in chapter 6); but most contemporary dialects of British English are more similar than different. In this discussion I will concentrate on those areas in which most of the differences are found.

Verb forms

In some non-standard dialects of English, including the one spoken by Mellors and the one studied by Jenny Cheshire in Reading (see chapter 1), the present tense *-s* form is not confined to the third person singular as it is in SE, but is added to all verbs. Cheshire's informants, for instance, said things like *we **has** a little fire*. In other varieties (the dialect of Norwich is an example), third person singular present tense verbs are not inflected with *-s*. In either case, the result is a regular present tense verb paradigm in which the verb form is the same all the way through (*I go(es), you go(es), it go(es), we go(es), they go(es)*). Since all subjects are followed by the same form of the verb, there is no overt marking of subject-verb agreement of the kind SE requires. Learners whose dialects are more regular than SE in this respect may therefore need to have the SE subject-verb agreement rule pointed out to them explicitly.

This is not the only case where the SE rules are less regular, and therefore less transparent in their logic, than the corresponding NSE rules. One of the side effects of standardization is to fossilize irregularities: because standard dialects are written and their rules are codified, analogical changes that would make them more regular may be inhibited by the perception that they are not 'correct'. Unwritten and uncodified varieties are more open to being regularized over time.

Another difference between SE and NSE verb forms relates to the past participle, which is used with auxiliary verbs 'have' and 'be' to form the perfect and the passive (e.g. *you've broken it* and *it's been broken*). English verbs can be regular or irregular: one way you can tell them apart is that regular verbs form the past participle with the same inflection—*-ed*—that is used to form the past tense (*he **played** football, he **has played** football all his life*), whereas irregular verbs may have different past tense and past participle forms (e.g. *you **broke** it/you have **broken** it*; *I **gave** a lecture/I have **given** a lecture*; *she **saw** you/she has **seen** you*). Or at least, they do in SE. In some dialects of NSE, one of these forms is used for both. So in London English you hear *She seen him* rather than *she saw him*; in Glasgow English you hear the opposite, *you've broke it* rather than *you've broken it*.

Negation

Forming negative sentences is an area in which there are potentially several differences between SE and other dialects. One that has shibboleth status is the ability of some NSE dialects to use an uninflected form 'aint' (or similar) where SE has present tense forms of the auxiliary verbs 'have' (*haven't/hasn't*) and 'be' (*aren't/isn't*). In the case of 'be', 'aint' can also be a main verb. For instance:

Table 2

Verb form	NSE example	SE equivalent
'Be' as main verb	*We aint friends*	We aren't friends
	She aint my friend	She isn't my friend
'Be' as auxiliary verb	*We aint talking*	We're not talking
	She aint talking	She's not talking
'Have' as auxiliary verb	*I aint finished it*	I haven't finished it
	He aint finished it	He hasn't finished it

Negative forms of auxiliary 'do' are also locally variable, with non-standard variants of SE 'don't'/'doesn't' including Yorkshire 'dunt' and Tyneside 'divvent'.

The other negation shibboleth is the so-called *double negative*, though linguists call this **negative concord**, because the rule does not limit the

number of negative markers in a sentence to two. Rather it says that
there should be **concord** (agreement): all the negatable elements in the
sentence should be negative. How many times negation is marked thus
depends on how many elements there are on which it is possible
to mark it. For instance:

> I aint done it (1)
> I aint done nothing (2)
> I aint never done nothing (3)
> I aint never done nothing to nobody (4)
> I aint never done nothing to nobody neither (5)

In SE, each of these sentences would have just one element marking
negation. This would be 'not' or 'n't' following 'have' in the first two
examples, and either 'n't' or 'never' in the others (*I haven't ever* or
I have never). 'Nothing', 'nobody' and 'neither' would become in SE
their non-negative counterparts 'anything', 'anybody' and 'either'.

Pronouns

SE does not make a distinction between the singular and plural forms of
second person pronouns: it uses 'you' for both. Originally, the singular
'thou'/'thee'/'thy' contrasted with plural 'ye'/'you'/'your' but over time
the singular forms were lost, as was the distinction between subject 'ye'
and object 'you' in the plural. But the change did not affect all English
dialects. Melvyn Bragg recalls that, growing up in Cumbria in the
1940s, 'we *theed* and *thoud* each other as if we had just got off the
Mayflower'; the linguist Katie Wales reports being addressed as 'thou'
by a bus driver in Sheffield as recently as 2000.[5] In some dialects, the
number distinction is made not by contrasting 'thou' to 'you', but by
contrasting 'you' to 'yous' or 'you all' ('y'all'). Scots and Irish English
have 'you'/'yous' (as does Liverpool English, which is influenced by Irish
varieties); southern US English has 'you'/'y'all'.

Another difference concerns the formation of **reflexive pronouns**.
In SE the rule for this is either, for first and second person forms, 'take
the possessive form and add -*self* or -*selves*' (as with *myself, yourself,
ourselves*), or, for third person forms, 'take the object form and add -*self*
or -*selves* (as with *himself, herself, itself, themselves*)'. Some dialects of

NSE have a more regular pattern in which the first of these rules applies to all pronouns. Hence the third person ones, like the first and second person ones, have *possessive + self/selves*, producing *hisself, theirselves*. In some dialects, too, the 'self' element of these pronouns is either *-sel* or *-sen*.

Other kinds of (non-personal) pronouns are also variable. Many non-standard dialects use 'what' rather than 'that' as a relative pronoun (e.g. *the book what I wrote*—which is quite logical given that other relative pronouns are WH- words, like *who* and *which*). Also quite common is the use of 'them' where SE has 'those', as in *put them boots somewhere I won't trip over them*.

What I have just given is not a full account of grammatical variation in British English, but even these few examples should be enough to make the point that standard and non-standard dialects are parallel systems, different in detail rather than in kind. All dialects have a grammatical structure that can be described in terms of rules (though all, including SE, have their exceptions and irregularities). The differences are largely superficial variations like the difference between 'canna' and 'cannot', 'isn't' and 'aint', or Norwich present tense verbs *I go, you go, he go*, standard English *I go, you go, he goes* and Reading *I goes, you goes, he goes*. If the proverbial Martian, unencumbered by any knowledge about the social status of their users, were asked to make a judgement on the relative linguistic merits of these variant forms, on what basis could he/she/it conclude that the SE ones were superior to the others? There is no linguistic basis for that judgement: when earth people make it, they are judging not the dialects but the people who speak them.

Dialect dilemmas

I said earlier that it would be difficult to dispute the educational importance of SE as the dialect of writing, and it does not seem likely its pre-eminence in that function will be seriously challenged in future. For writing, all dialects are not equal: centuries of development have given SE a stable writing system and a range of formal and technical registers which other dialects cannot match. It is true that other dialects could develop the same resources, but in the age of (standard) English as a global language it would not make much sense for them to do so.

Yet there are still, perhaps, some questions to be asked about the time and energy that is expended in the teaching and assessment of writing on the small differences that distinguish SE from NSE. It might be argued that the emphasis placed upon these differences is disproportionate to their actual significance. In my own sample of the writing of 13–16-year-old pupils from London schools—most, if not all, of whom must be speakers of NSE—what is striking is how few of their errors are attributable to grammatical interference from a non-standard dialect. It will be evident from the extracts I have reproduced that this is not because they are all highly accomplished writers. Many of them clearly have quite significant problems with writing, but these have far more to do with written sentence structure than with dialect.

As for why dialect differences should matter so much, a lot of commonplace observations on this subject will not bear close examination. For example, an A-level examiners' report recently commented that non-standard verb forms and negative sentences had prevented some candidates from communicating their meaning clearly. But this is disingenuous, as we can see if we examine some examples from my own collection:

And I did not write or do **no** work
She **like** being called Mrs Magrieola but her real name was Dagles
They **was** best friends

Inelegant though we might consider these sentences, there is surely no uncertainty or ambiguity about what they mean. If the examiners were honest, they would say: 'Non-standard grammatical forms rarely impede understanding, but since they are generally taken as indications that the writer is careless and ignorant, it is advisable to avoid them'.

This is a different kind of argument for paying attention to the minutiae of negation and subject-verb agreement: that if teachers do not do so, they are ignoring the reality of dialect prejudice and leaving pupils to suffer its consequences. But there is still a dilemma here, because educators should not be in the business of uncritically endorsing prejudice. Fortunately, the national curriculum does not only stipulate that pupils should be taught to use SE, it also says that they should be taught *about* dialect differences. Whether or not it was the curriculum designers' intention, this opens up a space in which the issues can be explored critically: if they know something about the history, structure and uses of English dialects, pupils as well as teachers can make up their own minds.

Registers

The following are all examples of real spoken or written English. Although I have taken them out of their original context, you will probably be able to guess roughly what the source of each one must be:

1. He's quite a lot of money tied up in erm property and things he's got a finger in all kinds of pies and houses and stuff a couple in Bristol one in Cleveland I think
2. And he's coming into the home straight now, and it's Chambers picking up the pace
3. Without prejudice to the overriding right to call for repayment on demand the overdraft facility will be available until further notice or until the agreed review date, which may be extended by mutual agreement.

Extract (1) is taken from a transcript of a conversation among friends; extract (2) is part of a transcript of a TV sports commentary on a sprint relay race; and extract (3) is part of a 'Terms and Conditions' leaflet issued to customers by a high street bank. This information probably comes as no surprise. But what was it about the language that enabled you to guess?

The answer may seem obvious: vocabulary. In casual conversation we talk about 'things' and 'stuff', whereas 'home straight' is from the vocabulary of racing and 'overdraft facility' is banking jargon. But while it is true that the vocabulary is part of what enables us to place these extracts in some kind of real-world context, the words do not do the job on their own. For example, we know the sports commentary extract could not be a newspaper report written after the race, though such a report probably would include the same key words and phrases (*home straight, Chambers, pick up the pace*). It is the *grammar* that tells this is commentary: specifically, the use of present continuous verbs to describe events as they are happening. The words in these extracts tell us what people are speaking or writing about, but it is the grammar working in conjunction with the words that tells us what **register** of language each exemplifies.

What is register and why does it matter?

A register is a variety of language which is associated with a particular context of use. Prototypical examples include 'journalese', 'legalese', 'bureaucratese', 'Parliamentary language', and 'baby talk'. From these examples it will be evident that a register is different from a dialect. Dialect variation is related primarily to characteristics of the speaker (like where s/he is from and what social class s/he belongs to). Register variation is related to characteristics of the communicative situation— things like the medium of communication (whether it is speech, writing or a hybrid such as email or online chat), its subject matter, its purpose, the social relationship between the producer and the recipient(s), its degree of formality and what professional or institutional setting it belongs to (e.g. school, the media or the law courts).

Although the actual term 'register' does not appear, the requirements of the national curriculum for English include a number that implicitly relate to pupils' understanding of register variation. For instance:[1]

- identify the characteristic features, at word, sentence and text level, of different types of texts (*KS4, Reading*)
- [understand] the differences between speech and writing [and] the impact of electronic communication on written language (*KS4, Language Variation*)
- write for a range of purposes [imaginative, informative, persuasive, analytical], drawing the forms for such writing from different kinds of text-types, e.g. stories, poems, diaries, memos, information leaflets, advertisements, editorial articles, reviews, reports (*KS3, Writing*)

The first of these requirements calls in general terms for attentiveness to the characteristics of different registers encountered in reading (the requirement appears specifically in a section about reading informational texts); the second focuses on the influence of the medium on the way language is structured, while the third suggests that pupils can be helped to 'write for a range of purposes' by looking at a range of written genres where language varies to reflect a combination of purpose, subject-matter and relationship to the reader.

These requirements do not say that 'pupils should be taught about the language of X, Y and Z' (e.g. 'advertising, bureaucracy and cookbooks'): there is no prescribed list of registers for them to study. Rather the aim is to make them aware of the general phenomenon of *variation*: what sorts of linguistic features may vary across different text-types, why they vary (that is, how variation relates systematically to factors like medium or purpose) and what effects are produced by varying them. Of course these general principles are best approached by looking at concrete examples. But the main objective is to develop an awareness of this kind of variation that pupils can apply in their own speech and writing and their encounters with texts of all kinds.

In earlier chapters I have touched on some features of a number of different registers in order to illustrate the nature and uses of particular grammatical phenomena (e.g. nominalization in tabloid headlines, or impersonal passive constructions in public notices and science writing). One register I have said much more about, however, is formal writing of the variety that is found in most academic (and other serious, non-fictional) texts. For teachers, knowledge about the characteristics of formal written English does have a special significance, because this is a variety of language pupils do have to be taught directly. It is also a 'powerful' register: being able to use it actively, as well as to read material written in it, is crucial to educational success. Understanding this register's characteristics, therefore, has a different status from understanding the characteristics of advertising or text-messaging or tabloid headlines.

My discussion here will both illustrate the general principles of register variation—how and why language varies with its context of use—and build on what has already been said about the characteristics of the formal written registers which are especially important in educational contexts. A good starting-point, since it is relevant to both these concerns (and is also picked out specifically for attention in the national curriculum), is the question of *medium*, and particularly differences between speech and writing. This subject has already been introduced (see chapter 5), but here I want to broaden that discussion and look more systematically at how and why the medium makes a difference.

Speech and writing

Let us return briefly to the piece of academic discourse that was analysed at some length in chapter 5:

> This seminar will take the findings of the Nuffield Inquiry and the government's literacy strategy as a starting-point for the exploration of the current situation in language education in the UK

You already know that this is originally a written text (I got it from a university noticeboard), but it is also possible to imagine it being spoken in a very formal situation where the speaker was working from a pre-written script: for instance, it could have been uttered at the seminar as part of the presenter's opening remarks. This illustrates that it is something of an oversimplification to talk generally about differences between speech and writing. In literate societies where most people use both, we find types of speech that are like, or based on, writing, and also types of writing (e.g. personal letters or diaries and today, email, text messages and online chat) which have many similarities to speech. The characteristics we consider typical of spoken and written language are not all determined by the medium in and of itself, but are also to do with the level of formality and planning. However, it is not wrong to think that, other things being equal, speech tends to be more informal and less planned, while writing tends to be more formal and more elaborately planned. These associations have arisen because each medium does have inherent characteristics which influence its most typical uses.

As I explained in chapter 5, one key difference concerns the kinds of processing spoken and written language require. Speech is inherently evanescent: it begins to disappear the moment it is uttered, and must therefore be processed by the hearer in real time. Writing consists of visible marks on a surface, and that allows readers to process it in different ways: to skim and scan, re-read, skip forward, and so on. While speech can of course be planned in advance, in many situations it is composed as the speaker goes along; though errors can be repaired, they cannot be erased. A writer by contrast can plan, draft and redraft, correct errors and edit for clarity. In printed or word-processed text no trace of this process need remain in the final product.

These considerations have implications for the kind of language that is likely to be used in each medium. Speech needs a higher level of *redundancy* to facilitate the process of composing and processing in real time. Hesitation, repetition, 'filler' words and phrases (e.g. *like*, *y'know*, *and stuff*) are all common in unplanned speech. The disparagement of these normal speech features as 'inarticulate' reflects most people's unconscious assumption that writing is or should be the norm for all language, but in speech they are helpful to the hearer as well as the speaker. A speaker who avoids them completely, even in very formal contexts (e.g. the lecturer who just reads out a pre-written text) can be very difficult to follow. Writers, however, must learn to be concise. Since readers do not have to process in real time, it becomes both possible and desirable to increase the information load.

In chapter 5 I illustrated the redundancy of informal spontaneous speech with a short extract of conversation:

A: And she didn't she didn't she didn't like Katy =
B: = no she didn't [like Katy
A: [she didn't like Katy at all

This also illustrates another difference. Speech tends to be more oriented to the *interpersonal* function of language, its use as a medium for making connections and facilitating interaction between people, whereas formal writing tends to be oriented primarily to the *referential* function, the use of language as a medium for transmitting information. The participants in the 'Katy' extract are not adding any new information by continuing to repeat the same point in the same words: rather they are establishing that point as something they (a) emphatically agree about and (b) are happy to go on discussing. Their behaviour reflects their social investment in the exchange, and in the interpersonal relationship it is helping to maintain. Even when participants in conversation are not socially close, their speech will tend to contain features which reflect the interactive nature of the proceedings.

Because speech usually involves participants who are present at the same time and/or in the same place, spoken language tends to be context-dependent, implicitly relying on the background knowledge participants share. Writing, conversely, is prototypically communication at a distance, with someone removed from you both spatially and temporally.[2] Communicating with others not immediately present was one of the main purposes for which writing was invented (the other being to reduce dependence on memorization). The implication, though, is that written language has to be interpretable without reference to shared context, and without the possibility of asking the writer directly for clarification: it needs to be *explicit* in ways most speech does not. Face-to-face with students in a classroom I could say: 'I want you to make one like this and bring it back here to show us at the same time next week', and they would know what I was talking about. But as a written note, the same instruction would be useless: without any shared context it is impossible to interpret most of the *deictic* terms referring to times, places and people (e.g. *I, you, one, this, back here, us, same time next week*).

Shared context allows speakers to make economies of expression. Though in terms of information content speech is often redundant and repetitive, structurally it tends to be less expansive, characterized by **economy features** such as the use of pronouns and other deictic terms which do not necessarily refer back to anything mentioned explicitly before (rather they refer to entities which are visible or otherwise knowable from the context), contracted verbs like *isn't, haven't*, and **ellipses**, sentences or phrases which are grammatically incomplete, like extract (1)'s *a couple in Bristol* (the full sentence form of which would be [*he's got*] *a couple* [*of houses*] *in Bristol*). Speakers can be economical in these ways because they know hearers can fill in the blanks. In writing, however, the onus is on the writer not to leave blanks. Writing is therefore characterized by **elaboration features** such as full sentences, full and often complex noun phrases, uncontracted verbs, and so on.

There is another important reason why written language tends to be more elaborate grammatically than speech: it is dependent on syntax for its structure and organization. Unlike speakers, writers cannot make use of the flexible and subtle resources of prosody—pitch, stress, pace, volume, tone of voice.[3] Speech is organized into prosodic units, marked off by pauses and intonation contours: they may or may not have the syntactic structure of complete sentences. Writing, however, relies on the sentence as its basic unit. It also makes more extensive use than speech of the possibilities of hierarchical structure or *hypotaxis*, for instance the use of subordinate clauses (spoken language is more likely to rely on coordination or *parataxis*). This reflects both the need for written information to be organized using syntactic rather than prosodic means, and the fact that writers generally have more time to do the planning complex hierarchical structures require. The table below summarizes these points and their consequences for the linguistic features which are typical of spoken and written language in their archetypal forms (i.e. informal unplanned speech and formal planned writing).

Table 1

Speech	Writing	Linguistic consequences
Evanescent: has to be processed (and often produced) in real time, with little planning or editing	Permanent: can be processed in a number of ways, planned in advance and edited before it is received by the reader	Writing generally has a higher information load: more lexical variation and more complex syntax; speech contains more repetitions, hesitations and fillers.
Interpersonally oriented: focuses on relationship between participants as well as content of what is said	Referentially oriented: primary focus is on conveying information	As above: vocabulary and syntax of writing reflect focus on information. They also reflect the more formal and impersonal relationship assumed to hold between writer and reader, and the absence of interactivity.
Context-dependent: speaker and hearer have shared spatio-temporal location	Context independent: reader may be remote from writer in time and space	Writing needs to be more explicit than speech: makes use of elaboration features (e.g. complex NPs), where speech makes more use of economy features (e.g. ellipsis, contraction, pronouns and other deictic terms).
Prosodic (organized using pitch, stress, pausing, etc.)	Syntactic (organized using sentence structure)	Unit of writing is the sentence; clause structure is more complex in writing, making more use of hierarchical relationships (i.e. subordination or hypotaxis). Units in speech more likely to be linked by coordination or just adjacency (parataxis).

Exploiting register variation: the case of advertising

It is not the case that all speech has all the characteristics listed in the first column of the table above and all writing those in the second column. Our understanding of the archetypal differences between speech and writing can be exploited to produce a variety of effects in either medium. I am writing this during a heatwave that has sent many Britons rushing to their barbecues, and prompted the government's Food Standards Agency to run a TV ad reminding us of the dangers of undercooked meat. Over a shot of sausages cooking on an open grill, the soundtrack plays the Three Degrees' song *When will I see you again?* After a few moments we see a sausage being prodded with tongs, revealing that it is burnt on the outside but practically raw inside. As the lyric 'when will I see you again?' plays repeatedly in the background, a written caption comes up on the screen: 'Sooner than you think if you don't cook it properly'.

This caption, though its medium is writing, has a number of speech-like qualities. To begin with, it uses the economy features of **contraction** ('don't') and ellipsis: ('sooner than you think' is an ellipsis of 'you will see me [the sausage] again sooner than you think'). The ellipsed information is supplied by the visual and the music track. Getting it also depends on resolving the puzzle of the deictic pronouns: as in informal face-to-face speech, the caption sends us to the surrounding context (rather than some previous bit of writing) to find referents for 'you' (the viewer) and 'it' (the sausage). Though we would generally tend to take 'you' in an advertisement to refer to us, the viewers, in this multimodal text (which juxtaposes image, music, sung words and written words) the caption does something more complicated. It transforms our understanding of the meaning of the song lyric, from *when will I* (the singer) *see you* (the unnamed lover) *again*, to *when will I* (the barbecuer) *see you* (this sausage) *again*. We then understand that the caption is part of a quasi-conversational exchange, answering the question 'when will I see you again' (a lyric whose relationship to sausages was obscure until that moment). The text as a whole thus simulates interaction on two levels (between the barbecuer and the sausages, and between the agency behind this campaign and the general public). One level is a joke, the other is the serious health message.

To understand these choices, it is relevant to know that British public information films have often been regarded as unnecessarily portentous and heavy-handed (classics of the genre include 'AIDS: Don't Die of Ignorance' and 'There's No Escape: Pay Your Car Tax!'). The barbecue safety message is part of a new wave which seems to be trying for a lighter touch. It uses humour, pop music and a conversational register of language to create the effect of informality and non-hierarchical social relationships.

For somewhat different reasons, commercial print advertising often exploits the same conversational features: the pseudo-interactivity of 'we', 'you' and **interrogatives** which position the reader as a partner in the 'exchange'; the informality of contraction and ellipsis, and deictic terms which are disambiguated not by previous text but by reference to either background knowledge or the picture element of the advertisement. For instance:

> We're reducing salt in our food faster than you can say 'sodium
> chloride' (*Marks & Spencer*)
> Adore Rubicon Mango? Then try new mouthwatering Rubicon
> pomegranate juice drink (*Rubicon fruit juice drinks*)
> Designed with attitude (*Mazda car*)
> What's a boundary? (*Lexus SUV*)
> It'll grow on you (*Futon Company sliding table*)
> Tired of wandering round warehouses full of boring 3-piece suites?
> (*Scandecor classic sofas*)

It would not however be accurate to say that these features are characteristic of all advertising, because the nature of the product being advertised (and the advertiser's perception of what kind of people might buy it) has a strong influence on the linguistic choices of advertisers. For example, it is common for advertisements for beauty products to draw on the register of science, which is not at all conversational: it is highly formal and impersonal, often complex in grammatical structure, makes extensive use of technical vocabulary and may make use of numbers, percentages and formulas. Here is an example of these features being exploited in an advertisement for hair conditioner:

Double action Nutri-Repair Conditioner: no more heartbreak for dry hair.
NEW ELVIVE ANTI-BREAKAGE WITH OMEGA CERAMIDE
1. Smoothing action: your hair feels softer and looks smoother on
    the outside.
2. Anti-breakage action: hair is more resilient and harder to break.
Up to 95% less breakage from brushing from the 1st application.
ELVIVE, tailor-made technologies for every hair need.
BECAUSE YOU'RE WORTH IT.

The more personalized language of other types of advertising does
creep in here, particularly in the familiar catchphrase of the L'Oreal
brand, *Because you're worth it*. But most of this text is pseudo-science
rather than pseudo-conversation: notice not only the vocabulary (*anti-
breakage, Omega Ceramide*) but also the use of nominalizations and
long, extensively-modified NPs (*double action Nutri-Repair Conditioner;
Up to 95% less breakage from brushing; tailor-made technologies for
every hair need*). It is also noticeable, however, that the text is not
organized in full sentences. Some economy features are used in most
advertising texts, because one constraint on their producers is what
you can get into the limited time or space available (in this case a
double-page spread which is largely taken up by a photograph of a
lustrous-haired celebrity, captioned 'This is no movie. This is science.').
I have chosen to discuss advertising partly because it is a perennially
popular topic for classroom teaching, but also because it raises
interesting issues about the concept of register. Some commentators
have questioned whether advertising actually has a distinctive register,
or whether the distinctive thing about it is its mixing and reworking of
a whole range of registers to serve the purpose of persuading particular
consumers to buy particular products. Certainly there is wide variation
in the kind of language advertisers use. There are radio and TV
advertisements which do not just borrow features from everyday
conversation, but directly simulate it. There are also, however,
advertisements which draw from the opposite end of the spectrum,
using a self-consciously 'literary' register (e.g. Guinness's 'surfer' ad
which quoted *Moby Dick*). And beauty products are not the only ones
that are advertised using features borrowed from scientific or technical
registers: the same strategy is common in advertising for health products,

household appliances and cars. At the same time, an advertisement that borrows from scientific registers is still distinguishable from a piece of actual science writing (no scientist would write about, say, *friendly bacteria*). The borrowing is selective and strategic, making the text overall a patchwork of different influences.

The only constant feature of advertising is its purpose: how that translates into concrete linguistic choices about, say, economy and complexity, degree of formality, how much and what kind of specialized vocabulary to use, will depend on what is being sold to whom—the subject-matter, the audience and the social relations implied by these— and on the constraints and possibilities of the medium (TV, radio, print, etc.). The point is, though, that by considering how these factors come together in any given case, you can generally give some account of why certain linguistic choices have been made. The same is true of all texts, whether or not they are readily labelled as exemplars of a single, well-defined register.

Register choice and critical language awareness

This way of thinking about registers—not as fixed templates which have been or have to be followed to produce a certain type of text, but as the more fluid outcomes of calculations about a series of variables such as medium, purpose, topic and audience—has the advantage of encouraging a 'critical language awareness' approach. Rather than stopping at the observation that register X is 'conventional' or 'appropriate' in a certain context, we can ask what makes it appropriate, and even question whether it really is appropriate.

In the world beyond the classroom there are real and sometimes difficult issues about the appropriateness of certain registers—particularly those in which experts and representatives of powerful institutions communicate with the public at large. In a modern democratic society, what is the 'appropriate' register for this sort of communication? How complex and how formal should it be? What kind of relationship with the recipient should it imply?

Below I reproduce a piece of legal language which, however, is not usually addressed to lawyers: it is the caution which police officers in England are legally obliged to give when they arrest someone.

> You do not have to say anything unless you wish to do so, but it may
> harm your defence if you do not mention when questioned
> something which you later rely on in court.

Although it is delivered orally, the language of this caution is remote
from ordinary speech, and that means it is not easy for a hearer to
process in real time. The vocabulary is not especially difficult (though it
is markedly formal, selecting for instance 'wish' rather than 'want', and
'harm' rather than 'hurt'), but the syntax is more complicated. Normal
speech economy features like contracted verb forms are pointedly
avoided; elaboration features like the added 'do so' in 'wish to do so'
make the utterance longer and more unwieldy. The embedded clause
'when questioned', positioned before the object of the preceding verb
'mention', is very un-speechlike, as is the placement of the adverb before
the verb in 'later rely on in court' (a more normal spoken order would
be either *rely on later in court* or *rely on in court later*). The whole thing
seems almost designed to make understanding it more difficult than it
needs to be, and research has suggested that many or most recipients
do not fully understand it.[4]

It might be argued that in a democracy, it is not acceptable for a
caution informing people of their legal rights to be expressed in a form
that they are likely to find incomprehensible. Yet against this it could be
argued that using simpler and more informal language (e.g. *you don't
have to say anything if you don't want to*) would be problematic both
legally and socially. In legal terms, a caution informing people of their
rights needs to be maximally explicit; in social terms it needs to embody
the authority of the law, while also acknowledging the gravity of the
situation for the recipient and treating him or her with due respect
(bearing in mind that s/he is innocent until proven guilty). Simple informal
language would offend against these principles, for it could be taken as
overly casual, or patronizingly basic, and therefore disrespectful. Social
considerations exert a powerful influence on language-use: because of
this, the most socially appropriate register in a given situation may not
always be the one that is easiest to understand.

We can apply the same kind of reasoning to a debate that is
perhaps a bit closer to home. Imagine that you are asked by a pupil
why s/he should not save time in a GCSE exam by using the conventions

of text-messaging in her/his answers (a practice recent examiners' reports complain vociferously about). Rather than just giving the most obvious answers ('because it's not appropriate/you'll lose marks/you're supposed to show you can write in academic English'), it ought to be possible to have a principled discussion of whether the examiners have sound reasons for their complaints, or whether they are just expressing a knee-jerk prejudice against a perfectly good way of writing.

Such a discussion would involve relating the specifics of the case to the factors that generally contribute to register variation: the conditions in which a text is produced and received, its subject-matter and purpose, and the level of formality or distance that characterizes the relationship between producer and recipient. It could be pointed out, for instance, that because of the nature of the medium and the (informal, equal) social relationships which are generally associated with it, text-messaging relies heavily on shared context and interactivity, and makes extensive use of economy features like ellipsis and contraction. Pupils could be asked to consider whether a register with these characteristics is well-suited to the purpose of conveying their ideas to an unknown GCSE examiner who is reading their work at a distance and cannot interact with them. They should then see that the problem with exam answers that read like text-messages is not that they are unconventional, or full of slang and bad spelling: the key issue is (in)explicitness, the fact that text-messaging as a mode of communication is (for good reasons) about economy, whereas academic writing demands (for equally good reasons) the opposite, elaboration.

SMS-language is one of several recent technologically driven innovations (others include internet chat and to a lesser degree, email) which can be thought of as hybrids of speech and writing. The medium in each case is written/graphic, so that messages are processed like writing, but the main uses of texting, chat, and some kinds of email are more like the traditional uses of speech—spontaneous and minimally planned social interaction between people who know each other and have a lot of shared context to draw on. These developments underline that the medium as such is not the only factor to be considered when thinking about the impact of new technology. Social relationships, and the purposes communication serves within those relationships, are the most important influence on the use we make of language.

Languages

There has never been a time in its history when English did not coexist with other languages spoken by significant communities of people—beginning with the Celtic languages of the ancient Britons, and continuing with languages spoken by later groups of migrants, such as Norse, French, Flemish, German, Chinese, Russian, Polish, Yiddish, Italian, Irish, and Romany. The tradition has continued: in London, one of the world's most culturally and linguistically diverse cities, a 2000 census of schoolchildren's first languages recorded approximately 300 different language names. In the much smaller town of Rotherham, in Yorkshire, a recent survey found 12 different languages in use.

One consequence of this diversity is that most teachers will at some point find themselves teaching pupils for whom English is an additional language. The standards for Qualified Teacher Status require all trainee teachers to be able to work effectively with EAL pupils, and recent recommendations suggest that three areas of linguistic knowledge are particularly relevant in that connection:[1]

1. Knowledge about how second/additional languages are learned, and about the linguistic development of bi- or multilingual individuals
2. Knowledge about the social and cultural contexts in which first or **community languages** are used, and the functions they fulfil for individuals and groups
3. Knowledge about English which teachers can use both to monitor EAL pupils' progress in learning the language, and to assess the linguistic demands of classroom tasks so that if necessary extra support can be given to EAL pupils.

Before turning to these areas of knowledge, though, it is important to make the point that linguistic diversity in the classroom is exactly that—*diversity*. The group of learners who are variously labelled 'EAL', '**bilingual**', 'pupils from diverse backgrounds', etc., are not only diverse in the sense that they belong to a range of different communities and collectively speak and/or write many different languages other than English. They are also diverse in their relationships to those languages and to English. Consequently it is something of an over-simplification to speak in general terms about their needs as a group.

It is certainly an oversimplification to use the terms 'bilingual pupil' and 'EAL pupil' as if they were interchangeable. A bilingual pupil is any pupil whose **linguistic repertoire** (I explain this term in more detail later) includes more than one language. Not all children in that category need English language support in school. Some may have acquired both English and another language before beginning formal education; their proficiency in English may be no less than the proficiency of their monolingual classmates. EAL pupils, by contrast, are those who have not had enough exposure to English to develop the level of proficiency which would be normal for English-speaking children (either monolingual or bilingual) of their age.

Within the EAL category there is also considerable variation. Some EAL learners are British-born children from established minority communities which have maintained the use of languages other than English for most purposes; others are migrants or refugees whose families have only recently arrived in Britain. Depending on age and circumstances, some may already have received extensive schooling in their countries of origin, while others may have had little or no education. Their parents or carers may be fluent in English or they may speak no English at all. There are also differences in their economic circumstances, and in the cultures of the communities they belong to. What these learners have in common—the fact that they are learning English as an additional language—should not obscure these differences, which may be just as significant in educational terms.

'First' and 'second' languages

Unless prevented by impairment or total isolation from other language-users[2], all children will acquire, during the first few years of life and without formal teaching, the spoken language or languages to which they are regularly exposed through interaction with their caregivers. Although there is still debate on the subject, most linguists and psychologists hold some version of the belief that the ability of human children to acquire languages in this way depends on an innate predisposition—what the popular writer Steven Pinker has dubbed 'the language instinct'.[3] According to this view, young children are primed with knowledge about the structure of human languages. This prompts them to look for certain kinds of patterns in the language that is actually used to them, and enables them to construct the rules which allow native speakers to use the language productively. Over time, however, this ability diminishes. Some theorists speak of a 'critical period' for language acquisition, a window of opportunity that gets smaller as time goes on and finally closes around the onset of puberty. After that, people can still *learn* languages, but they cannot *acquire* them in the way young children do.

The terms 'first' and 'second' language are often used to mean 'acquired' and 'learned'. It follows that an individual may have more than one 'first language', if s/he has been exposed to more than one in early childhood—and the term 'additional language' is used in recognition that people may subsequently learn more than one 'second language'.

There is a lot of academic debate about how far second-language learning resembles first-language acquisition, but everyone agrees that there are some differences. These are clearest when the comparison is between children acquiring first languages and adults learning second or additional languages. We know, for instance, that whereas all developmentally normal children acquiring a first language (L1) will achieve full fluency in speech, there is far more variation in outcomes among adults learning a second language (L2). Many adults will not achieve full fluency, and even those who do will almost always speak with an identifiably foreign accent. For adults, outcomes are influenced by factors like their motivation to learn and their level of education, whereas for children acquiring the spoken form of L1 these do not make any difference.

The understanding that children have a special ability to pick up languages is sometimes used as an argument for beginning foreign language teaching at an early stage of schooling. But that proposal rests on a failure to distinguish between acquisition and learning, and between different kinds of learning situations. First language acquisition occurs over several years of continuous exposure to a language or languages in natural situations. That is quite different from trying to learn a foreign language in classroom conditions, where you may only be exposed to it for an hour or two a week, and will have nothing like the intense, one-to-one interactions that take place between babies and their carers. Older children are actually better than younger ones at this kind of classroom-based learning.

The learning situation of most EAL pupils is different from either of the situations just outlined. On one hand they have not had sufficient exposure to English to acquire it naturally at the normal time for first language acquisition; on the other hand, since they are learning English in a society where it is the majority language, they will be exposed to it not only in classroom English lessons, but also in all other lessons, in informal interaction with peers, and in the course of other everyday activities. This kind of situation tends to produce high levels of both motivation and opportunity for L2 learning: within around two years, most children will be able to function well in everyday spoken interaction. That, however, does not mean that they will be able to use the L2 equally effectively for all the other purposes that are important in education. Learners who have already achieved conversational fluency in English may still need support in other areas.

This continuing need for language support in certain areas reflects the difference between two sets of language skills, which the researcher Jim Cummins has dubbed 'BICS' (Basic Interpersonal Communication Skills) and 'CALP' (Cognitive Academic Language Proficiency).[4] Cummins's distinction (which has been very influential, though it is not without its critics) can be related to the differences we examined in the discussion of (informal, unplanned) speech and (planned, formal) writing in chapter 9. Informal face-to-face speech, the kind that BICS relates to, has several characteristics that make life easier for language-learners. For instance, it tends to have low information density—there is a lot of repetition and redundancy—and because it is context-bound, the verbal message is usually reinforced by nonverbal cues such as gesture, gaze and facial expression. In addition, informal speech relies heavily on frequently used vocabulary items and grammatical structures that are easy to process.

In formal academic writing, by contrast—and speech-registers which resemble it—the learner faces a much greater challenge. Nonverbal information is drastically reduced, and information density increased; there is a much higher incidence of uncommon words, and the preferred grammatical structures are more complex. Cummins's point is that learners who function perfectly well in informal speech situations may still have difficulty with educational tasks involving language that is more complex and less context-bound. These are the situations for which BICS is insufficient, and learners need what he terms CALP.

CALP is not acquired naturally by anyone: it has to be developed in L1-users too. However, Cummins's research suggests that the process takes longer in a second language. L2-users may take between five and seven years to catch up with the academic language proficiency of their L1-using peers. If educators are not aware that there is typically a time-lag between developing age-appropriate levels of BICS and CALP, they may mistakenly attribute academic underachievement among apparently fluent L2-users to non-linguistic causes (for instance, classify them as having special educational needs) instead of offering the linguistic support which these pupils still in fact need.

The benefits of bilingualism

Cummins's arguments about BICS and CALP were developed in the context of North American debates on bilingual education, an approach in which pupils' first languages are used as the medium for some teaching. Supporters of this approach argue that language is a tool for thinking as well as communication: providing some teaching in pupils' first languages, in which academic proficiency develops more quickly, allows them to learn at a higher level than they would be able to if they were taught only in their second language. In Britain, where all EAL pupils are taught in mainstream classes, there is no debate on bilingual education as such, but there is discussion of whether and how it benefits pupils if their first languages are maintained and developed alongside English.

Like bilingual education in North America, this is a matter of some public controversy. In England (Wales is for obvious reasons a rather different case), public discussions of bilingualism are influenced by the

fact that the majority of English-speakers are themselves monolingual and regard 'one speaker, one language' as the norm. Many perceive second-language learning as a difficult task in which only the most academically gifted succeed. Consequently, there is a belief that the best course of action for children of immigrant families and minority communities is to abandon other languages and concentrate on English. When former Home Secretary David Blunkett made a speech along those lines, suggesting that immigrants should speak English to their children at home in order to avoid disadvantaging them at school and in later life, he was making the common assumption that language-learning is a sort of 'zero sum game': that our minds contain a finite space for it, and if too much of that space is filled with (say) Punjabi, there will be insufficient room for English. Another common belief is that expecting children to deal with two languages at once can only confuse them and lead to low levels of skill in both.

Most experts believe, however, that these are misconceptions, promoted by people with no experience of living life in more than one language, and no understanding of what is normal in other societies. Around the world, bi- or multilingualism is more common than the kind of monolingualism most British English speakers regard as normal. In many societies it is unremarkable for children to become literate in more than one language and/or in a language other than the one they speak. A recent doctoral research study conducted in Watford[5] found 5-year-olds of Pakistani ancestry routinely learning to read in three different languages—English, Urdu (the national language of Pakistan) and classical Arabic (the language of the Koran). While some of these children also had spoken Urdu as their first language, others were native speakers of Pahari (a related but different language). These 5-year-olds, then, were learning to read three languages, none of which was the written form of their natively acquired spoken language. They were also learning more than one script: unlike English, Arabic and Urdu do not use the Roman alphabet, and are written right to left. Far from being confused, however, these children displayed a high level of conscious awareness about different languages, scripts and cultural literacy-learning practices.

Research evidence also suggests that bilingualism and biliteracy can enhance skills in both languages, and have positive effects on educational attainment more generally. A study in Hackney, East London, found that 11-year-old learners whose home language was Gujarati and who, like the Watford children, had learned to read in Urdu and Koranic Arabic, outperformed their monolingual peers in tests of reading in English. Another London-based study found that Portuguese-speaking students who attended Portuguese mother-tongue classes were significantly more likely than those who did not to obtain 5 A*-C grades at GCSE.

Linguistic repertoires: how languages function

Some of the research studies I have just referred to were conducted partly in community-run 'supplementary' schools set up to support children's learning of community languages. The term 'community language' refers not only to the language a community speaks natively, but to any language that fulfils important functions for it. In many cases it is not the community's native language which will be taught in a community school, but rather the language or languages that are used for reading and writing. Once again, it cannot be assumed that what is true for British English speakers (who use the same language, English, for both speech and writing) is the rule in all other communities. In many communities there is a division of functions—and different communities may assign the same language different functions.

For instance, Punjabi, a language spoken in the Punjab region on the India/Pakistan border (and by large numbers of Asians in Britain) has a written form which is used by Indian (usually Sikh) Punjabis; but Punjabi speakers who are Muslims and live in or have roots in Pakistan learn to read and write in Urdu, not Punjabi. (Like other Muslims around the world, they also often learn to read Koranic Arabic.) In other cases a different language is used for speaking and writing because the spoken language has no codified written form. This is true of many (though not all) creole languages. Creole speakers in many parts of the Caribbean have traditionally been taught to read and write in the European language to which the creole is related, e.g. English or French, which is also used as the official medium of instruction in schools.

These examples illustrate a general, and important, principle. Language-users in all communities make use of a **linguistic repertoire**, in which different kinds of language conventionally fulfil different functions. In the British English-speaking community, as we saw in chapters 8 and 9, most people's repertoire includes some range of dialects and registers. The average person makes some use of both standard English and a localized non-standard spoken variety: SE is used in writing, while SE and NSE forms are used variably in speech to produce a range of more and less formal styles. Most people also draw on a repertoire of linguistic registers as they shift between different media, topics, addressees and situations (e.g. sending a text message to a friend versus writing a business letter to a client). In bi- or multilingual communities, the principle that different forms have different functions is exactly the same—but instead of assigning the functions to different varieties of the same language, as monolingual British English-speakers do, these communities may assign them to different languages. Where a monolingual would use *styleshifting* or change of register to indicate a shift in formality or subject-matter, a bilingual might use **codeswitching** —alternation between languages.

It follows from this is that a 'bilingual' is not necessarily someone who can do all the same things (e.g. speak, understand, read, write) with equal proficiency in every language that forms part of their repertoire. When languages fulfil different functions, you do not have to be able to use all of them for everything. The point is rather that your overall repertoire needs to be able to cover all eventualities. For children of migrant communities, though, that range of eventualities is increased and their repertoire has to expand to cover it. For instance, literacy in English is clearly indispensable for schooling and for life in Britain, but it is not by that token a substitute for literacy in community languages, since children may need to correspond with relatives overseas, or to be able to read important religious texts in another language. Maintaining community languages, and developing literacy in them, is also regarded by many parents as a vital part of maintaining cultural traditions and giving children a sense of their identity and history.

Teachers do not always have a full picture of their bilingual pupils' linguistic repertoires. Researchers working in community language schools frequently report that the mainstream schools attended by the community's children have little or no knowledge of what those children are learning elsewhere: teachers may not realize, for instance, that pupils are able to read in another language. That is a pity, since a fuller understanding of what bilingual and EAL pupils are capable of might help to counteract certain perceptions of them which are both inaccurate and damaging. For example, a study investigating the experiences of Chinese pupils who had recently entered British schools found that because they spoke very little English, most teachers had low expectations of their work, and they were also seen by peers as easy targets for bullying. The Chinese children became more and more withdrawn: but whereas the school interpreted this as a sign of their lack of confidence, the Chinese-speaking researcher found they were frustrated by having their limited English equated with limited intellectual ability. The following extract from an EAL pupil's recollection of starting school in London suggests that this kind of frustration is not uncommon:

> The fist day a went to school I was scared. I could not speak English and had a hard time doing all the [*indecipherable*] So the made me do some more easy work like colouring a pictuer and then we went to break I sat down on a bench and all of the class was looking at me and they try to help me with my English so I was not scared and then at lunch time people help me pick what I whated [*wanted*] and I was happy then I got sad when I to go home and I learn more English word so I was OK as the time went on I was learn new word and I still learn new words and I got the work that the class got so I was happy.

Looking at pupils' writing

It is not clear exactly how much time has elapsed between the experiences recounted and the composition of the text reproduced above, but at this point the writer's main difficulties are the same ones we have encountered when looking at the writing of non-EAL pupils—in particular, uncertainty about how and where to mark sentence boundaries. The errors that are more typical of L2 learning are those that relate to inflection. The writer several times uses an uninflected form of the verb where an inflected one is needed ('they try[ied] to help me . . .', 'people help[ed] me. . . ', 'I was learn[ing] new word') and the occasional plural inflection is missing also ('new word[s]'). This kind of morphological simplification is a common phenomenon in second language learning, reflecting the fact that inflectional systems take time to sort out, and the information they carry is often redundant in context, so that a hearer or reader will still get the gist without them. For instance, in 'I was learn new word' readers are unlikely to think that the writer means just one rather than many new words.

Simplification also affects syntactic operations. In a long narrative by another EAL pupil, Geeta, we find: *Raj came to see Angley's dad he said 'why you killed my dad'*. Here Geeta is applying a reduced form of the English rule for making WH- questions: she takes the WH- word and puts it at the beginning of the sentence, but does not follow the part of the rule which requires subject-verb inversion after the WH- word (which in this case would also require the insertion of the appropriate form of 'do', yielding *why did you kill my dad?*). Children acquiring English as a first language also go through a stage when they form WH- questions in this way: again, if you have the WH- word at the beginning to signal that something is a question, the rest of the rule is somewhat redundant.

This example illustrates the general point that many errors made by L2-learners are not random, but rule-governed and systematic. Rather than learning through imitation, learners go through a more active process of constructing and then applying rules which reflect their current reasoning about the way the language works. Clearly, nobody teaches them these rules: if a learner is taught grammatical rules they will be the ones an adult native speaker would follow. And in most cases, the L2-learner's rules are not the ones that apply to the equivalent structure in their L1 either. What learners like Geeta construct is a system in its own right, known technically as an *interlanguage*.

For Geeta, a school-age child learning English in an English-speaking environment, this interlanguage will almost certainly be transitional: as she amasses more evidence about how English grammar works, she will eventually arrive at the rule that is used by the adult/native speech community. Many researchers believe that direct teaching (e.g. correcting interlanguage forms) has very little effect on this process, and that the role of teachers is not so much to teach the language as to ensure that learners are provided with conditions that promote their own learning—for instance, exposure to language that is comprehensible but not too simple, and opportunities to use the language for interaction.

What languages are like: similarities, differences and relationships

One implication of the innatist view of first language acquisition, mentioned at the beginning of this chapter, is that at some abstract level all human languages must be very similar. The brain of a newborn infant does not know if it will be called upon to acquire English, Chinese or Swahili, but we know that children will in fact acquire whichever one (or more) of these they hear around them. However different they seem, therefore, these languages must all be structured on the principles that children are innately predisposed to apply.

Even people who are sceptical about the innatist view would accept that there are features (called **universals**) which are found in every language that has ever been investigated. For instance, all languages have both consonant and vowel sounds; all languages have words, and a distinction between nouns and verbs; all languages have constituent structure and the grammatical property of recursion (the 'Russian doll' or 'House that Jack built' principle that allows us to go on producing more and more levels of structure in a phrase or sentence). All languages also have ways of expressing concepts that are fundamental to human experience and interaction, such as time and space, existence and possession, the difference between one and more than one (number) and between the speaker, the spoken-to and the spoken about (person). Because human languages have many things in common, learners who have acquired one language already know a lot about what to expect from another, and can use their existing linguistic knowledge to support their learning of additional languages.

Of course languages can be more and less similar. Linguists have a number of ways of classifying the world's languages. One is on the basis of 'genealogy': some groups of languages show similarities because they are historically descended from a common ancestor. English, for instance, belongs to the Germanic subfamily of the large Indo-European group of languages. It is closely related to other Germanic languages such as Dutch, German and Danish; it is more distantly related to the Romance languages whose parent was Latin (they include French, Spanish, Portuguese and Italian), Celtic languages like Welsh and Gaelic, Slavic languages like Polish and Russian, and many languages of the Indian subcontinent, such as Bengali, Hindi, Urdu, Punjabi and Gujarati. By contrast, English is not genealogically related to Arabic (a member of the Semitic **language family**), Basque (an 'isolate' unrelated to any known language), Turkish (Altaic) or Chinese (Sino-Tibetan).

Other ways of classifying languages are less concerned with reconstructing their family trees than with identifying their structural 'type' (a sort of linguistic analogue of blood group, in that there are only a limited number of possibilities). One classification system is based on the normal order of the constituents subject, verb, and object. Another classification system that was popular in the 19th century was based on how much and what kind of inflectional morphology languages had: at that time some scholars believed that languages with complex inflectional systems (like Latin) were superior to those that made no use of inflections (like Vietnamese and Chinese).

Linguists today do not believe that any language or type of language is inherently superior or inferior to any other. (As I have already said, most believe that at a deep level they are all variations on a universal theme.) Nor do most contemporary linguists believe that the characteristic structures of your native language determine (or limit) how you think. The linguist Roman Jakobson once observed that languages differ not in what they *can* do but in what they *must* do: the rules of grammar make different things obligatory in different languages, but the fact that something is not obligatory does not mean it is not possible. For instance, French and German speakers are obliged, if they address another person using a second person pronoun, to indicate—by choosing either the familiar or the polite form (French *tu* or *vous*, German *du* or *Sie*)—whether they regard the addressee as an intimate, an equal, a social superior or an inferior. Modern standard English does not require that choice, since there is only one second person pronoun. Would anyone seriously suggest, though, that because of this difference in grammar, the English think less about status differences than other Europeans?

The beliefs people hold about different languages and the judgements they make on their relative merits are like the judgements they make on different dialects of the same language: what is really being judged is not the language but the people who use it. Unfortunately, many people do place languages in a hierarchy of value, which is related to the social characteristics of their speakers (like their nationality, their race and their status as immigrants). Thus people may view the ability to speak French or German (languages whose users in Britain are mainly educated white professionals or tourists) as a sign of intelligence and culture, while according no such respect to the ability to speak, say, Bengali (whose users in Britain are mainly relatively poor, non-white Bangladeshi immigrants). If we were willing to rank languages on criteria like whether they have educated speakers, a codified written form, a rich literary heritage, a history of being used in prestigious functions, etc., Bengali would be up there with French, German and English; but it is devalued in the British context because its speakers are perceived to be of low social status.

Because language is closely connected to personal and group identity, any devaluation of a language will be experienced by its users as devaluing *them*. Few teachers would ever deliberately do this, but it can happen inadvertently, through a lack of awareness and understanding. Of course teachers working in linguistically diverse schools cannot be expected to know everything about every language used by every pupil: the point is rather that they should have some awareness of what there might be to find out. Working effectively with EAL pupils requires both an understanding of their needs in relation to English, and a willingness to acknowledge and accord value to the other language(s) in their repertoires.

Notes

INTRODUCTION

1 Confederation of British Industry, *Working On the Three Rs*, (CBI, August 21, 2006).

CHAPTER 1

1 Mary Evans, *A Good School*, (London: Women's Press, 1991).

2 Quoted in Deborah Cameron, *Verbal Hygiene*, (London: Routledge, 1995), p.94.

3 Department of Education and Science, *A Language for Life*, [the Bullock Report] (London: HMSO, 1975), p.170.

4 *The Times*, March 17, 2003, *Daily Mail*, March 19, 2003, *Telegraph*, November 3, 2004, *Independent*, June 9, 2005.

5 Debra Myhill, 'Ways of knowing: writing with grammar in mind', *English Teaching: Practice and Critique*, 4(3): 77–96, 2005, p.79.

6 Paul Tench, 'What grammar is actually for', *Subject Centre Grammar Supplement*, (Southampton: Subject Centre for Languages and Linguistics, 2001), p.17.

7 Jenny Cheshire, *Variation in an English Dialect*, (Cambridge: Cambridge University Press, 1982).

8 Katherine Perera, *Children's Writing and Reading*, (Oxford: Blackwell, 1984), p.12.

9 Richard Andrews, Carole Torgerson, Sue Beverton, Terry Locke, Graham Low, Alison Robinson, and Die Zhu, 'The effect of grammar teaching (syntax) in English on 5–16-year-olds' accuracy and quality in written composition', (London: EPPI-Centre, 2004).

10 See e.g. Richard Hudson, quoted in 'Grammar for writing', *NATE News*, September 2005; Debra Myhill, op. cit; Dominic Wyse, 'Grammar for writing? A critical review of empirical evidence', *British Journal of Educational Studies*, 49(4): 411–27, 2004.

11 Department for Education and Employment, *English Department Training Materials*, (London: DfEE, 2001), p.106.

12 See Deborah Cameron, *Verbal Hygiene*, (London: Routledge, 1995).

CHAPTER 2

1 Wasyl Cajkler and Jane Hislam, 'Trainee teachers' grammatical knowledge', *Language Awareness*, 11(3), 2002, pp.170–1.

2 Answers/comments:

Word	Class	Comments
Teaching	Noun	In this sentence it isn't a verb, but what some grammarians call a 'gerund', a noun made out of the *-ing* form of a verb. You could put a determiner and adjectives before it, e.g. *her best teaching*; you could make it plural/possessive (*the teachings of Buddha*, *teaching's advantages*).
Fun	Noun/Adjective	This is occupying a slot that both nouns and adjectives can go in. You may have thought it 'described' *teaching* and was therefore an adjective: that's a bad argument, but there are better ones. For some (younger) speakers fun *can* inflect like an adjective—you can say *that was the funnest/most fun party* or *she thought of a really fun thing to do*. But it also passes many noun tests: it doesn't have a plural form but does have a possessive, and it can be preceded by determiners/adjectives (*the most incredible fun I ever had*). So either answer is OK if you gave good reasons.
Shot	Noun	The word can be the past tense form of the verb 'shoot', but here it is preceded by the determiner 'a', you could make it plural and add adjectives (*several loud shots*): so it's clearly a noun.
The	Determiner	More specifically, definite article.
Dark	Adjective/Noun	Preceded by 'the' here, it looks like a noun. But on inflectional criteria it looks more like an adjective (*darker, darkest*, not **darks*). Interestingly, many adjectives can go in this 'the __' slot, e.g. *defend* <u>*the indefensible*</u>', *take* <u>*the rough*</u> *with* <u>*the smooth*</u>'. Adjective may ultimately be a better answer, but noun is also reasonable.
He	Pronoun	One of the closed class of personal pronouns.
Recycled	Verb	Past tense ending makes this unambiguous.
Beer	Noun	*Not* an adjective, despite 'describing' (premodifying) *bottles*. You can't say **beerer, *beerest* or *the bottle was beer*; you can say *beers, beer's* and *the beer was flat*. Conclusion: 'beer' is a noun.
Bottles	Noun	Plural ending is the obvious clue here.
Would	Modal	Member of the closed class of modal auxiliary verbs.
Brilliantly	Adverb	Passes all adverb tests (movement is not totally free but could move to at least one other position, the end).
With	Preposition	
Your	Pronoun	Possessive form of the 2nd person pronoun 'you'.

CHAPTER 3

1 *Voiceless* and *voiced* are technical terms in phonetics, the study of speech sounds, and they refer to the difference between sounds made with the glottis

vibrating, which are voiced, and sounds made without this vibration, which are voiceless. The easiest way to 'get' this difference is to put your forefinger against your throat while saying a long, continuous zzzzz sound, moving your finger around until you feel the vibration of your glottis. Keep your finger where it is, and switch (smoothly, without pausing or taking a breath), to saying sssss. The vibration will stop. Now switch back to zzzzz and feel the vibration start up again. You won't have had to change the position of your lips or tongue to do this, because the presence or absence of voicing is the only difference between /s/ and /z/. (Try the same thing with /v/ and /f/. Which one is voiced?)

2 <s> uses carets to show that the enclosed symbol represents a **grapheme**—a unit of spelling; /s/ uses slashes to show that the enclosed symbol represents a **phoneme**—a unit of sound.

3 Links at http://www.edstud.ox.ac.uk/research/childlearning/learningliteracy.html.

4 The answers, with some comments:

Anti + clock + wise. *Clock* is a noun; *anti-* is a prefix meaning 'against' as in *antiracist, antihero*; *-wise* is a suffix meaning 'in this manner/direction', as in *otherwise, stepwise*.

Inter + nation + al + ism. *Nation* is a noun; *inter-* is a prefix meaning 'between', as in *interleaved, interpersonal*; *-al* is a suffix for making adjectives from nouns, as in *global, regional*; *-ism* is a suffix denoting an ideology or belief system, e.g. *communism, catholicism*.

Parliament + ary. *Parliament* is a noun; *-ary* is a suffix for making adjectives from nouns, as in *elementary, sedimentary*. You may have experimented with treating *-ment* as a **morpheme**, an affix for making nouns from verbs. In the original French it was exactly that (*Parliament* comes from *parlement*, 'speaking'), but in modern English we treat *parliament* as a single unit of meaning rather than decomposing it into a verb plus noun.

Kidult + hood. Here your question will be, why not *kid + ult + hood*? The answer is that the *-ult* is not a separable unit. *Kidult* is a blend, not a compound, and functions as one unit.

Vil + ifi + cation. The 'vil' part of this is a variant of the adjective *vile*. *-ify* (here spelt *-ifi*) is a suffix forming verbs from adjectives or nouns with the meaning 'to give something [the quality denoted by N or Adj]' (e.g. *glorify, prettify*), and *-(c)ation* is a suffix used to form abstract nouns (e.g. *beautification, glorification*).

Scandal. Despite ending in what might look like the adjective-forming suffix *-al*, *scandal* is a noun (quick test: you can make it plural with *-s*) and consists of one morpheme only.

Dis + advantage + ous. *Advantage* is a word (it can be both a verb and a noun); *dis-* is a prefix that negates whatever follows, as in *disqualify, disconnect*, *disreputable; -ous* is an affix for forming adjectives from nouns, e.g. *pompous, riotous*. Interesting factoid about *dis-* words: though English speakers will generally interpret them as carrying the meaning 'negative', there are quite a few that have no 'positive' counterpart. You cannot for instance be **gusted, *gruntled, *hevelled or *mayed*.

Slime + ball. A compound made from two nouns—and denoting not literally a ball made out of slime but a person the speaker considers 'slimy' (cf *oddball*, denoting a person the speaker thinks eccentric).

Supercalifragilisticexpialidocious. A trick question: being nonsense, this word cannot necessarily be expected to break down into meaningful sub-units, and not all of it does. There are however bits of it that do constitute separable units: *super-* for instance, a prefix meaning 'over' or 'transcending', as in *supermarket* and *supersize*; and the *-(c)ious* at the end, from which we know that whatever else it is, this word is an adjective, like the ones it rhymes with in the song: *atrocious, precocious*. The sequence *fragil(e) + ist + ic* is hard to extract a meaning from, but structurally it is possible to analogize it to real sequences of morphemes like *ideal + ist + ic*. The *ex-* of *expialidocious* could be the Latinate prefix *ex-* meaning 'out of', as in *exhume, extract*.

CHAPTER 4

1 There is an exception to this generalization: where the object is a **reflexive pronoun**, like 'herself' in *Jane cut herself*.
2 See Kate Clark, 'The linguistics of blame', in Michael Toolan (ed.), *Language, Text and Context*, (London: Routledge, 1990).

CHAPTER 5

1 Like other phrases, prepositional phrases can consist of just their head, a preposition, as in *she fell **down*** or *she walked **along***; but the ones relevant to this discussion have a more extended structure where they consist of a preposition followed by a noun phrase, as in *she fell **down the stairs*** or *she walked **along the road***.
2 MAK Halliday and JR Martin, *Writing Science*, (Pittsburgh: University of Pittsburgh Press, 1993).

CHAPTER 6

1 These examples come from data collected in Singapore by Jakob Leimgruber.
2 Caribbean creoles are the end result of a process which began with enslaved Africans learning a simplified (**pidgin**) form of a European language, such as English or French, which was used both for (limited) communication between European masters and slaves and as a medium of interaction among slaves

themselves, given that they usually did not share a common African language. In the Caribbean, reliance on pidgins led over time to them becoming the main languages acquired natively by children, and they were gradually elaborated to become the creole languages whose modern forms are spoken in the region today. In Singapore, by contrast, the (colonial) situation made it necessary or desirable for non-English speakers to learn English, but did not prevent them from using their own first languages or transmitting those languages to their children. Singapore English remains a learned language for many speakers, whereas creoles in the Caribbean are most speakers' native languages.

CHAPTER 7

1 The verbs are underlined, the clause boundaries are marked with slashes and italics are used to indicate the features (e.g. infinitive-marker *to* and subordinating conjunctions like *while* and *because*) that mark the clause as a subordinate clause.

> Bobby <u>went</u>/ *to* <u>get</u> his football from the garden/ *because* he <u>forgot</u>/ *to* <u>bring</u> it inside earlier that day/ *when* he <u>was playing</u> football with his brother. /So he <u>opened</u> the door in the kitchen/ and <u>came</u> out/ it <u>was pouring</u> with rain/ he <u>looked</u> for it/ and after a few moments he <u>saw</u> it. /He <u>ran</u> /*to* <u>get</u> it/ *while* he <u>was running</u>/ he <u>slipped</u>/ and <u>fell</u> on the muddy grass/ or <u>did</u> he./ He <u>looked</u> at the place/ [*where*] he <u>fell</u>/ there <u>was</u> no stones there only grass/ it <u>was</u> something else/ he <u>wiped</u> his hand through the grass/ and the grass <u>went</u> to the side/ and he <u>saw</u> a handle and a boxed shaped door or maybe a trapdoor.

There are a couple of things that might have confused you. The 'after' in *and after a few moments . . .* is not being used as a subordinating conjunction but is just an ordinary preposition; we can tell this because it is followed by a noun phrase ('a few moments'), not a clause, which would have a verb (e.g. *and after he had waited a few moments*). In *he looked on the place he fell*, 'he fell' is a relative clause postmodifying 'the place', but you might have missed that because there is no explicit relative pronoun (if there were it would be the one I have inserted, 'where'). In the last, long clause you might have been tempted to subdivide before the coordinators 'and' and 'or'. But there are no verbs after these coordinators, so what they are doing here is not coordinating clauses; rather they are coordinating NPs (*a handle* <u>**and**</u> *a box-shaped door* <u>**or**</u> *a trapdoor*). 'And', 'or' and 'but' can all link words and phrases as well as clauses (e.g. *friend or foe, slowly but surely*): the general rule is that they should link units of the same kind.

CHAPTER 8

1 Peter Trudgill, *The Social Differentiation of English in Norwich*, (Cambridge: Cambridge University Press, 1975).
2 The study is reported in a doctoral thesis: Susan Fox, *New Dialect Formation in the English of the East End of London*, (University of Essex, 2004).
3 An interesting study of how, when and why school-age speakers make use of ethnic varieties which are not 'theirs' is Ben Rampton, *Crossing: Language and Ethnicity among Adolescents*, (London: Longman, 1995).
4 'All raait! It's a new black-white lingo', *Sunday Times*, December 11, 2005.
5 Both cited in Katie Wales, *Northern English*, (Cambridge: Cambridge University Press, 2006), p.182.

CHAPTER 9

1 The first point is a direct quotation, but the other two are my own summaries of longer sections.
2 Obviously there are exceptions, many of them created by modern technology. I can leave a friend in Australia a phone message she may not get for many hours, or send an email or text message to someone sitting in the same room.
3 Some features of written language simulate spoken prosody, though they do not have its subtlety: for instance punctuation marks, conventions such as underlining or italicizing to indicate emphasis, and—an interesting recent example—the emoticons or 'smileys' used in computer-mediated communication to convey that a contribution is meant to be humorous or ironic.
4 Thanks to the forensic linguist Frances Rock (personal communication) for this information.

CHAPTER 10

1 See Jill Bourne and Rosie Flewitt, 'Teaching Pupils from Diverse Backgrounds: What do Trainee Teachers Need to Know?', (Teacher Training Agency, 2002). My three-point list is distilled from those recommendations that relate directly to *linguistic* knowledge (other important issues addressed by Bourne and Flewitt include the induction of newly arrived pupils, working in partnership with EAL specialist teachers and classroom assistants, and building relations with pupils' families and communities).
2 There have been cases relatively recently of children who did not acquire language because prolonged and severe neglect deprived them of spoken input. Until the development of sign languages in the late 18th century, profoundly deaf children were also in this position. Their inability to hear speech made it impossible for them to acquire language.

3 Steven Pinker, *The Language Instinct*, (Harmondsworth: Penguin, 1994).

4 See Jim Cummins, 'BICS and CALP', http://www.iteachilearn.com/cummins/bicscalp.html.

5 This and the following examples are all taken from summary reports produced by the Community Languages Research Group based at the Institute of Education, London and made available on NALDIC's (National Association for Language Development in the Curriculum) website. http://www.naldic.org.uk/docs/research/bilingual.cfm, accessed August 28, 2006.

Further Reading

References to all the sources I have cited and/or quoted can be found in the notes to the relevant chapter. This section suggests some follow-up reading on the main topics covered in this book.

Guides to English grammar
David Crystal, *Rediscover Grammar*, 3rd edn, (Harlow: Longman Pearson, 2004).
Comprehensive but accessible; a good choice if you want to look up facts, terms and definitions.

Resources for teachers
Richard Bain and Elspeth Bain, *The Grammar Book*, (Sheffield: NATE, 1996).
This is a set of classroom materials for KS3. A supplementary volume was published in 2003.

The LINC Materials: Materials for Professional Development, (Dept. English Studies, Nottingham University).
These materials were produced as part of a professional development initiative called Language in the National Curriculum (LINC) in the early 1990s. Their anti-prescriptive approach was controversial, however, and the authorities of the time refused to publish them. They were nevertheless widely circulated and very popular with teachers. Though they are no longer easy to get hold of, the LINC materials can still be found in some resource centres and libraries.

The **Qualifications and Curriculum Authority** (QCA) has published a number of reports and other materials dealing with grammar. The ones listed below can be ordered in print form, or downloaded free of charge, from the orderline section of the QCA's website (www.qca.org.uk).
Making Connections: Grammar and Meaning, 2004.
Written by Debra Myhill, this short paper contains some useful observations about teaching grammar for writing in a way that is not decontextualized and mechanical. Also good on formality and register or text-type.
Introducing the Grammar of Talk, 2004.
A helpful resource for thinking about grammar in relation to speaking and listening objectives.

The Grammar Papers: Perspectives on the Teaching of Grammar in the National Curriculum, 1998.

Standard English
James Milroy and Lesley Milroy, *Authority in Language: Investigating Standard English*, 3rd edn, (London: Routledge, 1998).
A book about where notions of 'correct' and 'incorrect' English come from, and what their consequences are in education and society. Good on speech-writing differences and standard/non-standard dialect differences; also good on the facts of language discrimination in the UK and USA. The book is aimed at professionals like teachers and speech therapists as well as students of linguistics and language history.

Tony Crowley, *Standard English and the Politics of Language*, (Basingstoke: Palgrave, 2003); Tony Crowley (ed), *Proper English: Readings in Language, History and Cultural Identity*, (London: Routledge, 1991).
These two books take a less exclusively linguistic view of standard English, making use of historical scholarship and critical theory to put debates on the subject in their political and cultural context.

John Honey, *Language is Power: The Story of Standard English and its Enemies*, (London: Faber, 1993).
Honey's view represents the opposite end of the political spectrum from Crowley's. Linguistically this is not a very well-informed book, but it is a good distillation of a particular set of arguments.

Regional and ethnic varieties of English
Joan Beal, *Language and Region*, (London: Routledge, 2006).
Introduction to regional accent and dialect variation in Britain, with examples, maps and activities.

For information on the creole varieties used in Britain, a good reference is **Mark Sebba's British Creole Resources** webpage, which includes some classroom materials. http://www.ling.lancs.ac.uk/staff/mark/resource/resourcs.htm. If you are interested in pidgin and creole languages more generally, an accessible introduction is
Ishtla Singh, *Pidgins and Creoles: An Introduction*, (London: Arnold, 2000).

Two interesting books about young people's language-use and its relationship to ethnic identity are
Roxy Harris, *New Ethnicities and Language Use*, (London: Palgrave Macmillan, 2006).

Ben Rampton, *Crossing: Language and Ethnicity among Adolescents*, (London: Longman, 1995).

Information on other languages spoken in the British Isles and the communities that use them can be found in
Safder Alladina and Viv Edwards (eds), *Multilingualism in the British Isles*, (London: Longman, 1991).
though this needs to be used with caution, because the picture has changed since it was published: some newer language communities may not be covered, and some of the information on more established communities will be out of date.

Register and textual variation
Maggie Bowring, Ronald Carter, Angela Goddard, Danuta Reah, and Keith Sanger, *Working with Texts*, (London: Routledge, 2007).
General introduction to the practical linguistic analysis of texts, which is designed to work with a series of more specific introductory-level books called *The Language of* . . . Their topics include the language of advertising, magazines, television, websites, literature, poetry, conversation, children, humour, politics, war, work and sport. Written by various authors, they contain activities that can be used directly with English language A-level students (or adapted for others).

Sharon Goodman and David Graddol (eds), *Redesigning English: New Texts, New Identities*, (London: Routledge, 1997).
This book is good on the relationship of English to new media and technologies, and on English as a global language. Written for the Open University, it is also well designed for independent self study.

The history of English
David Crystal, *The Stories of English*, (London: Penguin Books, 2004).
Good source of information, ideas and examples for teaching about change in English. Deals with regional and non-British dialects as well as standard English, and it is good on grammar as well as vocabulary. Much more comprehensive and reliable than 'story of English' books authored by media celebrities like Melvyn Bragg and Bill Bryson—and very readable in spite of its length.

The Oxford English Dictionary (OED) online
The *OED* is unlike most English dictionaries in being primarily historical—it tells you how words have developed over time (also where they originally came from and when they were first attested in writing) rather than focusing only on their current definitions. Exam boards recommend the *OED* as an invaluable resource for A-level teaching. The online version (which can be searched more quickly and easily than

the print one, though arguably it is less good for random browsing) is available in most academic libraries and many UK public libraries.

Language learning and linguistic development
Neil Mercer and Joan Swann (eds), *Learning English: Diversity and Development*, (London: Routledge, 1996).
Another volume in the Open University series, which focuses on the learning of English as a first, second, spoken and written language.

Patsy Lightbown and Nina Spada, *How Languages Are Learned*, 3rd edn, (Oxford: Oxford University Press, 2006).
Some of this will be of limited relevance for English teachers (as opposed to EAL or EFL specialists), but for anyone interested in language learning it is an informative guide—also concise, straightforward and practically oriented. It is mainly about second/additional languages but does include some material on first language acquisition.

Jean Stilwell Peccei, *Child Language*, (London: Routledge, 2006).

Glossary of Terms

Note: bold type is used for cross-referencing to other glossary entries.

Accent. Pronunciation.

Active voice. The alternative to the **passive voice**: if a sentence is not passive it will be active.

Additional language. Alternative term for **second language**, which acknowledges that a learned language may not be literally the second one a speaker learns; it could be the third or the thirteenth.

Adverbial. An optional constituent slot in sentences which can be filled by an adverbial phrase (e.g. *she arrived quite unexpectedly*) or a prepositional phrase (e.g. *she arrived in the morning*); typically adds information about when, where, how, or why.

Affix. Something that is added or fixed on to a **stem**: affixes can be either **inflectional**, used to make different forms of the stem-word (e.g. *cat~cats; play~played*), or **derivational**, used to make another word from the stem word (e.g. *cat~catty; play~playful*). Affixes added to the end of the stem are called suffixes, and affixes added to the beginning of the stem are called prefixes (prefixes in English include *un-, dis-, pre-, de-*). Some languages have *infixes*, affixes you put into the middle of a stem: in English this can be done with certain swear-words, e.g. *absobloodylutely, fanfuckingtastic*.

Agent. The doer of an action, e.g. *John killed the spider*. In **active** sentences, commonly appears in the grammatical **subject** slot.

Agent deletion. A feature of some **passive** sentences, whereby the **agent** of an action is not mentioned, e.g. *Your cat has been run over.* An **active** sentence would have to put the agent in the **subject** slot (though the subject could be vague and generic, e.g. *someone has run over your cat*).

Agreement. A phenomenon whereby the form of one constituent reflects the characteristics of another which it is linked to. In English, **subjects** and verbs have to agree in **number** and **person**, though this only overtly affects sentences in the present tense which have third person singular subjects, whose verbs are marked with an *-s* ending (this rule does not apply in all dialects). **Pronouns** agree in number, person and (for third person pronouns) gender with the noun phrase they replace or refer back to. (e.g. *my father wrote off his car and had to sell it for scrap*).

Aspect. A system of contrasts in the form of verbs, which relates to the 'internal temporal consistency' of an action or state—e.g. whether it is completed or ongoing, of long duration or no duration, recent or non-recent. In most dialects of English, verbs can be marked for **continuous** aspect (using auxiliary *be* + *-ing*) and for **perfect** aspect (using auxiliary *have* + *-en* or *-ed*).

Auxiliary verb. A verb which is not the main verb in a clause or sentence but precedes that verb; the verbs which are used in English as auxiliaries are *have* (used to mark perfect aspect), *be* (used to mark **continuous aspect** or **passive voice**) and *do* (used to make **negative** and **interrogative** sentences), plus the **modal** auxiliaries.

Bilingual. Term referring to a person or a community whose **linguistic repertoire** contains more than one language. (Though *bi-* means 'two', the term is also often used in relation to people and communities who use more than two.) It does not have to mean that both/all languages were natively acquired, nor that the user is equally proficient in both/all of them.

Blend. Word which is formed by 'blending' part of one word together with part of another, e.g. *breakfast* + *lunch* = *brunch*. Differs from a **compound**, which puts together whole words (e.g. *lunch* + *box* = *lunchbox*).

Clause. Grammatical unit containing a verb. Can be equivalent to a sentence, or can be part of a sentence that contains more than one clause. Clauses can be **finite** or **non-finite** and **main** or **subordinate**.

Closed class. Word class that has a finite number of items in it and cannot readily be added to. Closed classes in English include pronouns, determiners, prepositions and conjunctions. Closed class words are sometimes called 'function words' (contrasted with 'content words'), but they are not entirely without content or meaning (there's a difference between, say, *I* and *you*, *a* and *the*, *up* and *down*, *and* and *but*). In most cases, however, they are more predictable than open class words like nouns and verbs, and can more easily be omitted in 'telegraphic' genres like headlines and text messages.

Codeswitching. Alternating between different languages in the same interaction. Common among **bilingual** speakers.

Codification. The process of writing down the rules of a language system, e.g. dictionaries codify word meanings and spelling, and grammar books codify the rules of grammar and usage.

Community language. Term often used in Britain for a language other than English that serves important purposes for a minority community. It does not necessarily refer only to the first language which the community uses in everyday conversation (e.g. Classical Arabic is an important community language in many Muslim communities, whose members learn to read it in order to read the Koran, though in many cases their first language is not any variety of Arabic).

Comparative. Form of adjectives and adverbs, marked by the affix -*er* or by putting *more* before the adjective/adverb.

Complement. A constituent that follows verbs like *be, become, seem* and 'completes' a proposition about the **subject** of the sentence. Is usually a noun phrase or an adjective phrase, e.g. *James is **an arrogant twit**, James seems **exceptionally arrogant**.*

Complex sentence. Sentence containing one or more **subordinate clauses**.

Compound. Word formed by putting existing words together, e.g. *blackbird, whiteboard*. Generally has a more specific meaning than the same items not compounded (e.g. a crow is a black bird, but not a *blackbird*).

Concord. Another word for **agreement**.

Conditional. Name for the kind of sentence that has an 'if . . . then' structure. In English there is no special conditional form of the verb, but conditional sentences involve particular relationships between the verbs in the 'if' and 'then' parts of the sentence. For instance: *if he **tells** them, they **will** believe him; if he **told** them, they **would** believe him; if he **had told** them, they **would have** believed him*.

Conjunction. Something that joins grammatical units, particularly clauses and sentences, together: there are **coordinating** conjunctions (like *and*) which place the items linked in a non-hierarchical relationship—they are like items in a list—and **subordinating conjunctions** (like *because, whereas, although*) which place the items linked in a hierarchical relationship, where one depends on another.

Connective. Another word for **conjunction**.

Continuous. Aspect marked by using auxiliary *be* and the -*ing* form of the following verb, e.g. *I'm loving it*; *we were travelling at 30 miles an hour*. Indicates that an action or state was/is of some duration, persistent/repeated, or ongoing when something else happened.

Contraction. An economy feature shortening the forms of verbs, e.g. *she's* (uncontracted form *she is*), *didn't* (uncontracted form *did not*).

Coordination (adj. *coordinating*). Joining elements of structure together in a non-hierarchical way, e.g. with a coordinating **conjunction** like *and*.

Creole language. A language that develops from a **pidgin** as it becomes the main medium of communication for a community (and possibly the **first language** of their children). Creoles unlike pidgins are 'full' languages, but they generally preserve characteristics which reflect their pidgin origins, e.g. economical and transparent grammatical systems.

Declarative. Sentence that makes a statement rather than asking a question or issuing a command.

Degree modifier. Category of words such as *very, quite, rather*, etc., which can precede adjectives and adverbs to indicate the degree to which they apply.

Deixis (adj. *deictic*). Deictic terms have meanings which are not fixed but relative to the location in time and space and the participants involved in the communication situation. For example, the determiners *this* and *that*, spatial/temporal terms like *here*, *there*, *now*, *then*, and all **pronouns** are deictic. In speech, especially face-to-face, the information needed to interpret deictic terms will typically be available from context; in writing however it is necessary to ensure that the relevant information is provided explicitly in the text. This is something young writers often find difficult, since it requires keeping close track of what the reader can or cannot be expected to know.

Derivation (adj. *derivational*). Making words from other words.

Descriptive grammar. Account of a language's structure that aims to describe how the language works and what its users know about it, as opposed to making rules for how to use it 'correctly': contrasts with **prescriptive grammar**.

Dialect (adj. *dialectal*). Variety of a language that is distinguished from other varieties by features of its grammar and vocabulary. Most dialects are localized, i.e. they are distinctive to a particular place or region, but non-localized varieties like **standard English** are also technically dialects: their distinctiveness is social rather than local.

Dislocation. Moving a constituent out of its 'normal' position to emphasize it as the topic or the main point, e.g. <u>Cats</u>, *I hate them* or *he's always been mean, has <u>Fred</u>*.

Economy features. Features commonly used to save time and processing effort in situations where the participants have a lot of shared context (e.g. informal conversation): they include **ellipsis**, **contraction** and the use of unelaborated **deictic** terms.

Elaboration. The process of 'enriching' a language so it can be used for all purposes; this may require designing a writing system for it, borrowing or making new words (e.g. technical vocabulary), and developing styles and **registers** (e.g. academic, legal, religious, scientific) which did not previously exist.

Elaboration features. The opposite of **economy features**, found in more formal situations where participants do not have a shared context and need to spell things out explicitly.

Ellipsis. Grammatical incompleteness: constituents may be omitted if the hearer can reasonably be expected to supply them from context or the preceding discourse. For instance, [*it's a*] *nice day*, or *no I can't* [*lend you £50*].

Finite. A verb is finite if it is marked for **tense**, past or present. A clause is finite if it contains a finite verb.

First language. Language acquired through natural exposure to it in early childhood (it is possible to have more than one first language).

Gerund. Traditional name for a noun made out of the *-ing* form of a verb, e.g. *her singing is appalling.*

Grammatical. In linguistics, a sentence is grammatical if it conforms to speakers' tacit understanding of what is possible or impossible in a language. Not the same as 'grammatically correct'; e.g. *It's me* is grammatical in English although prescriptivists say it should be *it is I.*

Grapheme. Unit of spelling: in many cases a grapheme is a letter, but in some cases it is more than one (e.g. <th> in English is a grapheme: it functions as a single unit, representing a single sound rather than the two sounds /t/ + /h/). Learning to spell entails learning the correspondences between graphemes and **phonemes**, units of sound in speech. In English these relationships are fairly complicated, and some features of English spelling (like how plural or regular past tense endings are spelt) are related to **morphology** rather than sound.

Head. The word a phrase is built around (in some cases it may be the only word in a phrase).

Hypotaxis (adj. *hypotactic*). Way of organizing text that involves the use of subordinate clauses. Contrasts with **parataxis**.

Imperative. Used to issue bald commands like *duck!* Imperative sentences are formed using uninflected verbs, and they do not have to have a **subject** (though they can have a second-person subject, e.g. *you come here this instant!*)

Indicative. Used for statements and questions; contrasts with **imperative** and **subjunctive**.

Infinitive. The uninflected form of the verb, which can be preceded by 'to' (e.g. *I told him to go*). As its name implies, it is **non-finite**.

Inflection (adj. *inflectional*). Change in the form of a word to indicate a grammatical distinction, e.g. **number** (plurality), **tense**, **aspect**, possession. Most inflections in English are affixes, but some irregular verbs are inflected for past tense by changing their vowel (e.g. *sing~sang*).

Interrogative. A category of sentences which use syntax—inverting the normal order of the **subject** and verb—to convey a question: they may be *polar*, yes/no interrogatives or WH-interrogatives beginning with *what, which, when, where, why,* and *how.* Not all questions are interrogatives: in speech it is possible to convey questions using intonation rather than syntax, or in writing, to add a question mark to something that is grammatically declarative (*you know what I mean?*)

Intransitive. A verb is intransitive if it does not have an **object**. Some verbs are always intransitive (e.g. *be*); others can be either intransitive or transitive.

Irregular verbs. The ones which do not make their past tense just by adding *-ed.*

Language family. Group of languages descended from a common ancestor.

Levelling. The process whereby varieties whose speakers are in regular contact get more similar to each other: the sharpest differences are 'levelled out'.

Lexis (adj. *lexical*). Words, vocabulary.

Linguistic repertoire. The set of language varieties—different languages, **dialects**, styles or **registers**—which an individual or a community is able to use; often there are rules and conventions governing which varieties fulfil which functions.

Main clause. Clause that is **finite** and not **subordinate**: complete sentences contain at least one clause of this kind.

Modal auxiliary verb. There are nine of these: *can*, *could*, *shall*, *should*, *will*, *would*, *may*, *might*, and *must*. They come first in any sequence of verbs, and they do not have inflected forms. Their meanings are to do with possibility, necessity, permission and obligation.

Modality. Linguistic devices which indicate the degree to which a proposition is possible, likely, certain, etc. In English, **modal auxiliary verbs** are important indicators of modality.

Mood. Generic term referring to the **indicative**, **imperative**, and **subjunctive**.

Morpheme. Smallest unit of form/meaning. May be a word (e.g. *word* is a morpheme), or may be an inflectional or derivational **affix** found on many words (e.g. *-s* as in *words*, *-y* as in *wordy*, *-ness* as in *wordiness*).

Morphology. The study of the internal structure of words. One of the two main branches of grammar, the other being **syntax**.

Negative concord. Observed in many non-standard dialects, this is the rule that every element in a negative sentence that can be made negative, should be made negative, e.g. *He never did no harm to nobody*.

Nominalization. Condensing a proposition into a noun or noun phrase: very common in academic, scientific, and bureaucratic English, where we often find phraseology like our <u>*understanding*</u> *is* . . . rather than *we understand* . . . ; also common in headlines in the popular press.

Non-finite. Non-finite clauses have verbs which are not marked for past or present tense—they are either **infinitives** or **participle** forms. These are **subordinate** clauses, though in some literary writing they are used on their own to produce a 'stream of consciousness' effect.

Non-standard. Term applied to any dialect which has not undergone the process of **standardization**.

Notional definition. A definition that relies on intuitions about meaning rather than form, like 'a verb is a doing word' or 'a sentence is a complete thought expressed in words'.

Number. The distinction between singular and plural.

Object. A constituent, generally a noun phrase or **pronoun**, which follows a **transitive** verb. Some verbs have two objects (traditionally called 'direct' and 'indirect'), e.g. *she gave me a present*. If something is an object you should be able to construct a **passive** sentence in which it moves to the position before the verb and becomes the **subject**: for instance *a present was given to me* or *I was given a present*.

Open class. A word class that is open to the addition of new items: noun, verb, adjective and adverb are all open classes.

Optional variability. Characteristic of language whereby there is often more than one way to communicate the same thing, and this permits language-users to choose according to the demands of the situation (e.g. how formal or polite they want to be). Suppressing or reducing this variability is one of the goals of **standardization**.

Parataxis. Way of organizing text that depends on **coordination** rather than **subordination**.

Participles. The *-ing* and *-en* or *-ed* forms of verbs (traditionally called 'present' and 'past' participles, but in fact they have no **tense** and can both be used with **auxiliary verbs** in either tense).

Passive voice. Alternative to the more common **active voice**. In a passive sentence the grammatical **subject** is the entity which is semantically **patient**— not the doer but the 'done to'. The **agent** can be specified in a 'by' phrase following the verb, or there may be **agent deletion**. The verb is marked as passive by combining auxiliary *be* with the past participle form, e.g. *The spider was killed by John*.

Patient. A semantic role; the recipient or sufferer of an action (e.g. *John killed the spider*). In a **passive** sentence, appears in the grammatical subject slot.

Perfect. Aspect marked by using auxiliary *have* + the past participle form of a following verb, e.g. *she has gone*. Used to indicate that a past action/state is (still) relevant in the present.

Person. Three-way distinction between *I/we, you* and *he/she/it/they*—these first, second and third persons correspond roughly to the speaker(s), the spoken-to and the spoken about.

Phoneme. Unit of sound in the spoken form of a language.

Phrase. A unit of grammatical structure consisting of one or more words, but which is not a complete clause/sentence. Phrases are built around words of a certain class, e.g. noun, adjective, adverb, preposition. They can be replaced or moved as whole units.

Pidgin. Auxiliary second language improvised by speakers who have no common language so they can communicate for limited and specific purposes (e.g. trading). If maintained over a long period and/or acquired natively by children, a pidgin may develop into a **creole language**, with a more complex structure and a larger range of functions.

Postmodifier. Part of a noun phrase that comes after the head noun; can be a prepositional phrase or a relative clause, e.g. *the hostess <u>with the mostest</u>*; *the spy <u>who loved me</u>*.

Premodifier. Part of a noun phrase that comes before the **head**; nouns can be premodified by adjectives/adjective phrases, and other nouns, e.g. *<u>dangerous</u> dogs*, *<u>pet</u> dogs*.

Prescriptive grammar. Aims to define 'correct usage' in a language.

Progressive. Alternative name for **continuous aspect**.

Pronoun. Pronouns come in several sub-types: **personal** pronouns (e.g. *I*, *your*, *them*), *interrogative* and *relative* pronouns (the WH- words that are used to form interrogative sentences and to introduce **relative clauses**), *this/that/these/those* (a set of determiners which are traditionally called *demonstrative* pronouns) and 'indefinite' pronouns like *one, someone/ anybody/nobody*. Pronouns can go in subject, object and complement slots, where they substitute for fuller or more specific noun phrases (e.g. 'she' for 'Deborah Cameron' or 'someone' for 'a person I cannot/don't wish to identify more precisely').

Prosody. In speech, the use of pitch, stress, loudness, and tempo to convey information about the structure and meaning of utterances. (In writing, syntax and punctuation do these jobs.)

Received pronunciation (RP). High status British English accent, which signals that the speaker is educated but not what part of the country s/he grew up in.

Recursion. The 'Russian doll' principle which allows us to embed one grammatical unit inside another of the same kind (e.g. a sentence within a sentence or a noun phrase within a noun phrase): this means that in theory the sentence or phrase can be extended indefinitely, e.g. *this is the cat that ate the rat that stole the malt. . . .*

Reflexive pronoun. A pronoun that ends in *-self* or *-selves*.

Register. Variety of language associated with a particular institution or context of use, e.g. 'legalese', 'journalese'.

Regular verb. Verb that makes its past tense by adding *-ed*.

Relative clause. Kind of **subordinate clause** that is part of a noun phrase, e.g. *the house <u>that Jack built</u>*. May be introduced by a relative **pronoun**, e.g. *that*, *which*, *who*, *where*, etc.

Second language. Language which is not acquired through natural exposure in early childhood, but learnt at some later point (this may be either through formal instruction in a classroom or through 'immersion', i.e. living in the relevant community and using the language to interact with people; or it may involve a combination).

Semantics (adj. *semantic*). The study of meaning.

Standard English. Non-localized dialect of English used for most kinds of writing, and as a spoken variety by many educated/high-status speakers.

Standardization. The historical process whereby a dialect is selected to serve as a **supra-local** standard, and undergoes **elaboration** and **codification** to equip it for that role.

Stem. What an **affix** is added to.

Stratification. Sociolinguistic pattern whereby the proportion of standard to non-standard forms rises in parallel with the class status of the speaker.

Styleshifting. Sociolinguistic pattern whereby the proportion of standard to non-standard forms rises as the situation becomes more formal.

Subject. A constituent slot that needs to be filled (typically by a noun phrase or **pronoun**) in almost all sentences (**imperatives** are an exception). It is the constituent the verb agrees with and in English **declarative** sentences it usually comes before the verb (in interrogatives it comes after the first verb). In **active** sentences it is frequently associated with the role of **agent**—the doer of an action (e.g. *she felt his cheek with her fingertips*)—or 'experiencer' of a state or process (e.g. *she felt ill*).

Subject-verb agreement. See **agreement**.

Subjunctive. A **mood**, contrasting with **indicative** and **imperative**. Historically used to express wishes and hypothetical states, e.g. *God save the Queen, as it were, so be it*, the subjunctive only survives now in examples like these that have become stock formulas. No one today would say *My lottery numbers come up* meaning 'I wish they would . . .'

Subordinate clause. A clause that is not a main clause; sentences containing subordinate clauses are termed **complex sentences**.

Subordinating conjunction. May introduce a subordinate clause: examples include *if, because, though, when, that*.

Superlative. Form of the adjective made by adding *-est* to it or preceding it with *most*.

Supra-local. A form or variety that has currency beyond the immediate locality—either national (like standard English) or regional.

Syntax. The study of phrase and sentence structure. Syntax and **morphology** are the two branches of grammar.

Tense. A contrast relating to time which is marked on verbs: in English, the contrast is between past and present tense. **Non-finite** verb forms have no tense-marking.

Transitive. A verb is transitive if it has an **object**.

Universal. A feature, pattern or tendency found in all human languages.

Variety. 'Neutral' or non-committal term for a kind of language, e.g. a dialect, style, or register.

Voice. See **active voice** and **passive voice**.

Word class. Category of words defined by formal characteristics, e.g. what inflections can or cannot be added to them and what positions they can or cannot occupy in larger units. There are **open classes** and **closed classes**.

Word formation. Making new words from existing stock; deriving words from other words.

Zero conversion. Transferring a word from one class to another without altering its form, e.g. the noun *fish* becomes the verb (*to*) *fish*.

Index